INDIANS OF THE FOUR CORNERS

INDIANS OF THE FOUR CORNERS

The Anasazi and Their Pueblo Descendants

ALICE MARRIOTT

Drawings by
Margaret Lefranc

ANCIENT CITY PRESS
SANTA FE, NEW MEXICO

Cover design by Connie Durand

Book design by Mary Powell

Cover illustration: *Serpent, Tadpoles, Corn, Lightning, Eagle, Male Figure*, gouache by Milland Lomakema (Hopi), Blair Clark, photographer, Museum of Indian Arts and Culture/Laboratory of Anthropology, Santa Fe, New Mexico. Number 52796/13.

Printed on acid-free paper

Grateful acknowledgment is made for permission to reprint the following material.

Ruth L. Bunsel, for "The Growth of the Corn" and "Prayer Spoken While Presenting an Infant to the Sun," from *Zuni Ritual Poetry* in the Forty-Seventh Annual Report of the Bureau of American Ethnology; 1932, Government Printing Office.

Natalie Curtis, for "Corn-Grinding Song" and "Corn Dance Song," from *The Indians' Book*; copyright 1935, by Harper & Brothers; by permission of Paul Burlin.

H. J. Spinden, for "That Mountain Far Away" and "The Willows by the Waterside," from *Songs of the Tewa*; copyright 1933, Exposition of Indian Tribal Arts.

Library of Congress Cataloging-in-Publication Data

Marriott, Alice Lee, 1910–1992
    Indians of the Four Corners : The Anasazi and Their Pueblo Descendants / Alice Marriott ; drawings by Margaret Lefranc.
      p.   cm.
    Originally published: New York : Crowell, [1952].
    Includes bibliographical references (p.   ) and index.
    1. Pueblo Indians. 2. Indians of North America—Southwest, New—Antiquities. 3. Southwest, New—Antiquities. I. Title.
E99.P9M34   1996
979'.01—
                                95-50494
                                CIP

10 9 8 7 6 5 4 3 2 1

For *Judith* and *Patrick*
and *Pamela* and
Sidney, who joined their
family in that order,
and for *Ann,*
who was promised a book
long ago

CONTENTS

ACKNOWLEDGMENTS

A PARTIAL bibliography, which includes museum collections that have been consulted or visited, will be found in the back of the book. And a partial list of the persons who have aided in its preparations must include:

For the use of specimens and of previously unpublished material:

F. H. Douglas, Denver Art Museum, Denver, Colorado
Dorothy Field, Denver Art Museum, Denver, Colorado
Jno. B. Jackson, Santa Fe, New Mexico
Mrs. Maria Martinez, San Ildefonso Pueblo, New Mexico
Mrs. Leonidas Romero y Vigil, Nambé Pueblo, New Mexico
Mary Chiloquin, Beatty, Oregon

For editorial advice and assistance:

H. Marie Wormington, Denver Museum of Natural History, Denver, Colorado
Arminta Neal, Denver Museum of Natural History, Denver, Colorado
Judith Marriott, Fort Sill, Oklahoma
Sydney C. Marriott, Oklahoma City, Oklahoma
Margaret Schoonover, Nambé, New Mexico
Paul Coze, Phoenix, Arizona
Oklahoma Historical Society, Oklahoma City, Oklahoma

THE JOURNEY TO THE
FOUR CORNERS

FROM THE TIME of the earliest immigrants, all the New World peoples knew how to make string, and they all made it in the same way. They twisted two, four, or eight strands of fibers together into a single cord. (Our string, the kind that was invented in Europe, is usually made with three, six, or nine twisted strands.) All the early Americans knew how to make points and blades out of chipped stone, and they all had tame dogs, perhaps to help the men in hunting. And although they could not read or write, all the early Americans seem to have known the same stories, for we find certain tales told in the same way by peoples who are the whole length of the hemisphere apart.

These people were the ones we call today the American Indians. They called themselves different names in their own different languages, and most of the names meant "Men" or "People." They had never seen any other kind of human beings. When the Indians did finally meet white people, they thought the newcomers looked very strange.

We are still learning about the long, long history of the Indians before Europeans landed on the East Coast of the American hemisphere from Europe. Archeologists, who are scientists who study the past, are unraveling the story a little at a time. Because the archeologists are still working things out, we have to say "perhaps" and "possibly" about a lot of things connected with the early Indians. After all, the records the early people left us are in the forms of basketry and pottery and stone tools and weapons and paintings on the walls of caves and places of worship. They wrote no books that would tell us what they believed and how they felt. Instead of facts they bequeathed us artifacts, which are products of early art. From these, if we are wise enough, we can read their story.

Twenty thousand years ago there were people living only in the Old World. Both North and South America, the continents of the Western Hemisphere, were the homes of animals and birds that had never heard of human beings. We do not know the reason why half the world was uninhabited by man.

Twenty thousand years is only a breath of time in the history of the earth, for during the millions of years since our planet was formed the globe has changed its size and shape many times. If the earth is drawn nearer the sun by gravity, or is pushed away from it by the same force, or if a land mass cools and shrinks so that an ocean rises and spreads, the balance and shape of the earth are changed.

So it seems likely that at the time when humans were beginning to be, the Americas were at the bottom of an ocean, or were covered with ice, or possibly were blazing with volcanoes. At any rate, no one lived in the New World for a long time after there were people in Asia and Europe and Africa.

Then there came another change in the earth's form, and the land we call the Diomede Islands was heaved up above the surface of the Bering Sea by volcanic action. The new land did not take the form of islands at first. To begin with, a land bridge, or peninsula, stretched across the narrow body of water that now lies between Asia and Alaska, and the islands we see on our maps today rose above the rest of the land and formed a chain of mountains.

Land and sea, even that far north, were not as cold then as they are now. People could set out from the Asiatic mainland in canoes, or could walk overland along the seashore, and travel a long way to the east. In time, some people reached Alaska. Probably they were just wandering along with their families, hunting and fishing as they went, without any plans about where they were going or what they would do when they got there. It is likely that people went back and forth between Alaska and Asia as much as they wished for quite a long time. Even in modern times their Eskimo and Indian descendants on the opposite sides of the Bering Strait could visit one another.

The life of the early people was unchanged when the land bridge gradually sank into the sea, leaving some people on either side of the straits. What did make a difference to these people was that some of them on the American side found that there was more game inland than there was along the coast. They started to spread out and to wander over the American continents, looking for more food and better weather, since Alaska had turned cold by this time. As they went along the travelers had to change their ways of living to suit the new conditions they encountered.

In time, the people's customs changed so much that it was only their appearance that showed these first Americans were related to their Asiatic cousins. On either side of the Bering Strait lived people with yellow-brown or brown-brown or copper-red-brown skins, straight, coarse black hair, and black eyes. Many of these people had a little fold in each of their upper eyelids so that their eyes seemed to slant slightly upward, toward their temples. The men probably plucked out the few hairs that grew on their faces.

People who came from different parts of the Asiatic mainland, or who settled in different parts of the American continents, spoke different languages from the earliest times. Different groups had different religious beliefs, different social customs, and different ways of making their livings. They lived in different kinds of country so they ate different kinds of food, wore different kinds of clothing, and built different sorts of shelters. In fact, it is surprising, when you come to think about it, that they looked as much alike as they did and had even a few things in common.

As the Indians wandered away from Alaska, they followed the shape of the country and traveled along the seashore or through the valleys, where the walking was easy. Old Indian legends tell us that the people followed the sun southward. These Indians had no maps and no domesticated animals except their dogs. They had no metal tools, and they knew nothing about wheels. These things were invented long after the emigrants left Asia. The people journeyed on foot, and they carried their string utensils and stone weapons with them. When the wandering Indians found places where there were wild seeds, or berries and fruits, or nuts or acorns that were good to eat, they stopped for a while. Perhaps they camped overnight in some places and stayed for months or years in others. We still find the fire-blackened stones that rimmed their campfires and the tools and weapons people lost or discarded on the shores of the old lakes in the plains, or on the stone shelves of bluff shelters in the mountains.

They were families and groups of families, all traveling together. There were young men and women, who were strong and active. There were mothers and fathers with their children. And there were the oldest people to help take care of the babies. As the Indians traveled, new babies were born, and older people died. Young people grew up and married and had families of their own. Probably there were accidents with falling trees or rocks, and perhaps some of the men were hurt when they went hunting. People got sick, and the Indian doctors treated them and cured them. Each time there was a birth or a death or a sickness the whole group of people would have to stop for a while. Perhaps some of the strong ones became impatient and refused to wait, and hurried on, forming a new group of their own. Perhaps those who had stopped liked their resting place so well that they remained where they were for the rest of their lives, and their children and the children's children stayed there after them. All kinds of things must have happened to the journeying Indians, sometimes to hurry them forward and sometimes to delay them. Some people stayed in Alaska, and others traveled all the way to Tierra del Fuego, the southern tip of South America. Others settled in Nevada, while their friends went on into the Arizona mountains or the brush country on the edge of the Great Plains.

We can only guess at most of the things that happened to the people who followed the sun. However, archeologists are certain that by our year A.D. 11 there were Indians living in the country that now includes our southwestern states. In the region where the Rocky Mountains rise from the Great Plains, and the peaks and mesas (MAY-sahs) are separated from one another by deep canyons or wide dusty valleys, these people found a place to live, and because they lived there they developed certain crafts and skills and songs and prayers and beliefs. From northwestern Utah to northeastern Colorado, southward through New Mexico, and westward again into northern Arizona, spread the people we call today the Anasazi (Ah-nah-sah-zee), a name given them by the Indians of another tribe. It means: The Ancient Ones.

In time the Anasazi became a great people. They and their descendants have lived for two thousand years in the same mountainous part of our Southwest. The point where the corners of Utah, Colorado, New Mexico, and Arizona join today was the heart of the old Anasazi country. The Four Corners Area, as it is called now, is still a sacred place to the Anasazi descendants, the modern Pueblo (PWEB-low) Indians, who live along the Rio Grande (REE-oh-GRAHN-day) and in the mountains of northeastern Arizona. These Indians can trace their families back from mother to grandmother to grandmother's mother, all the way along the line to the Anasazi Ancestress-of-the-Whole-Clan, who first settled down beside a campfire of juniper sticks, somewhere in the future Four Corners, about the year 1000 B.C.

We really ought to be grateful to this old lady, and it is too bad we don't know her name. She probably was called Lone Pine Standing or Pink Flower Blooming or Water Falls from the Sky, because those are names like the ones the modern Pueblo Indian women have.

Old Grandmother and her family chose a perfect place to live if they wanted to leave behind them a record of the life they lived because their country provided them with certain raw materials. The climate of the Four Corners country is so dry that fur and feathers and buckskin and string and baskets and even human bodies do not always rot if they are buried in the ground. Instead, such things often dry up and are perfectly preserved so that later-comers may study them.

Wind and water have carved great natural caves in the walls of the canyons that cut into the sandstone and volcanic tufa mountains of the Four Corners. These canyons also divide the mesas, or tablelands, from each other. In these open bluff shelters the early people found protection from storms. There they stored their food and hid their treasures. In the open-faced caves they buried their dead and sometimes built and occupied huge cities.

Archeologists have been able to dig through layers of earth, stacked one above another like the layers of a cake, in the caves of the Four Corners Area. Between the layers, where there are bits of string and pieces of stone and other articles to show that the caves were occupied, there are levels of plain dirt to show when the people moved away for a while. By reading downward, the scientists can tell what happened in Anasazi and Pueblo Indian life as the centuries followed each other. The archeologists can tell when only Indians lived in the New World, from their baskets and pottery. Then they can see when Europeans entered the country, by the metal knives and tools they traded to the Indians. They can tell us when Indian pottery was replaced by European china and brass, and when tin cans were introduced into the Indian country. If you will look at the chart on pages 156 and 157 and read the tables from the top down, you can see how the archeologists have worked out the history of the Pueblo Indians and earlier Anasazi

Ancestress-of-the-Whole-Clan

history. This is how scientists are sure about the dates in Indian history:

Every tree that grows makes a growth ring for each year of its life, just inside its bark. The rings are formed outward from the heart of the tree. If there is a damp year, the tree grows well, and there is a wide ring to prove it. If the year is dry, the tree grows very little, and that year the growth ring is narrow. Between each pair of rings there is a dark line to show when it was winter and the tree did not grow at all.

Certain pines and other evergreens make the clearest records, and many such trees grow in the Four Corners Area. When trees grow in the same part of the country, their growth rings naturally are very much alike. When a young tree begins to grow, its inside rings show the same pattern as the outside rings of an old tree in the same area. If one tree is cut down and the other is left to grow, the living tree will carry on the growth pattern from the place where it stopped in the dead tree.

When the Anasazi cut trees for their early brush shelters, and later for house beams and lintels, they left other trees still growing. Centuries later, the Pueblo Indians cut the growing trees to use in building later dwellings. Archeologists learned that they could take samples of wood from old and new houses and match their ring patterns. The scientists could count the ring pattern of a tree that had just been cut, continue through the pattern of growth in the beams of a fifty-year-old house, and go on matching and counting from one building to another till they got to houses that were so old there was no wood left. Sometimes the archeologists got back to houses that were nothing but walls of sticks with mud plastered over them. The earliest tree-ring date is our year A.D. 11.

So we know positively when the oldest Anasazi houses were built in the Four Corners, and we know how the shapes and sizes and locations of the houses changed during the 1,276 years that the Indians lived in that area. We know what year the people built their great towns, and when they deserted them and moved southward through the mountains and along the river valleys; and we know where they settled at the end

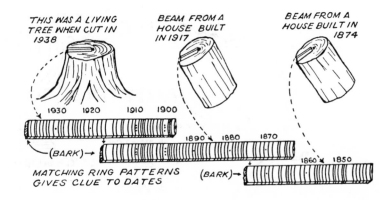

THIS WAS A LIVING TREE WHEN CUT IN 1938

BEAM FROM A HOUSE BUILT IN 1917

BEAM FROM A HOUSE BUILT IN 1874

1930 1920 1910 1900

(BARK)→

MATCHING RING PATTERNS GIVES CLUE TO DATES

1890 1880 1870

(BARK)→

1860 1850

of their second great journey, although we do not yet know why they followed the sun and the shape of the country to the south again.

Today we can drive over good roads to the mesa-top and cliff-side cities of Mesa Verde (MAY-sah VAYR-day), or to Chaco (CHAH-ko) Canyon; to the ruins of Puye (poo-YAY) and Tyuonyi (chee-YON-yee) on the Pajarito (pah-hah-REE-toe) Plateau; and to the deserted city of Aztec (AZZ-teck), which had one of the greatest places of worship of them all. We can see the outlines of the towns and the lines of stones that show the forms of the houses; we can see the tools and utensils, the clothes and weapons, and even the bodies of the people who lived in these places. Our government has saved and protected these precious things for us and sheltered many of them in National Park Service museums.

We can drive through the towns of the living Anasazi—the Indians we call the Pueblos, or townsmen. We can start in northern New Mexico, at the five-story town of Taos (TAH-ose), and go southward through San Lorenzo de Picuris (sahn lo-REN-zo day pick-cur-EES), San Juan (sahn WAHN), Santa Clara (SAHN-tah CLAH-rah), San Ildefonso (sahn EEL-day-FONE-so), Nambé (nahm-BAY), Tesuque (tay-SOO-kay), Cochití (coe-chee-TEE), Santo Domingo (sahn-toe doe-MEEN-goe), San Felipe (sahn fay-LEE-pay), Santa Ana (SAHN-ta AH-nah), Zia (ZEE-ah), Jemez (HAY-mess), Sandia (sahn-DEE-ah), and Isleta (iss-LAY-tah). Then we can turn westward, through Laguna

(lah-GOO-nah) and Acoma (AH-come-ah), to Zuni (ZOO-nee)
and the Hopi (HOE-pee) villages of Arizona: Bakabi (BAAH-
kah-bee), Hano (HAH-no), Hotevilla (HOTE-vil-lah),
Kiakochomovi (kee-AH-ko-tcho-MO-vee), Mishongnovi (mish-
ONG-no-vee), Moenkopi (moe-en-KOP-ee), Oraibi (o-RYE-bee),
Polacca (po-LAH-kah), Shipaulovi (Shee-PAH-lo-vee),
Shungopavi (shung-MO-pah-vee), Sichomovi (see-CHUM-o-vee),
and Walpi (WAHL-pee). In the modern Indian towns we see
the descendants of the Anasazi. They live in their own way,
by shaping the customs of their ancestors to meet the needs
of modern life.

Sometimes it is hard to tell where Anasazi life ends and
Pueblo Indian life begins. Some of the customs of the modern
Indians must be at least a thousand years old. For that reason,
all through this book references will be made to ''modern''
Anasazi and ''ancient'' Anasazi people, and the customs,
beliefs, habits, and traditions that they shared.

Archeologists make many other divisions in the periods of Indian history in the Southwest. They talk about the times of the Basketmakers: the people who had not learned to make pottery or were just beginning to discover it. They talk about the Pueblo One period, when cotton was introduced and turkeys were domesticated in the Southwest. Or they speak of the architecture of the Pueblo Two period, or the time when the people moved southward in Pueblo Three times, or when the Spaniards invaded the country in the Pueblo Four period. Archeologically speaking, the modern Indians are living in the Pueblo Five period.

THE CITIES OF THE
FOUR CORNERS

THE EARLY Anasazi, in the days when they traveled to their homes in the Four Corners, lived like seed-gathering, hunting peoples everywhere in the world. The Indians didn't build real houses then, and there was no one place they thought of as home. In their wandering days the Anasazi gathered their homes as they gathered their food—a stick here and a leafy branch there. At the end of each day's trip they piled the odds and ends together and covered the stack with brush or bark to keep off the rain and cold while they slept. In good weather the Indians probably slept outdoors, without cover of any sort.

Those customs changed after the Indians settled down in the Four Corners Area. One reason for the Indians' choosing that section may have been that they found brush and bark to build shelters on the mountainsides and mesa tops. The days were usually sunny, for the climate is dry most of the year in that section. Even in winter the days were warm, and if the nights became unbearably cold the people could go into the bluff-shelter caves and at least get out of the wind.

The early Indian settlers had few tools. They knew how to make weapons, and they carried hammerstones, knives, spears, and spear throwers with them for hunting, as well as to protect themselves against their enemies. The Anasazi had never heard of metal, so they made all their blades and points of stone. Tool-making and house-building went together all through Four Corners history. Whenever a new tool was invented, there was a change in the way the Indians lived.

As long as the only tools they had were hunting weapons, the Anasazi built hunters' shelters. They threw little heaps of brush and bark together beside their campfires. In windy weather the Indians weighted the outer branches down with slabs of stone. Once in a while an archeologist is lucky enough to find one of these stone circles somewhere on a mesa top or in a remote mountain meadow. Weapon points and knife blades might be nearby, lying where people lost or discarded them centuries ago.

These early camps in the open were small. A few families were all clustered together so they could help one another with hunting and gathering. If many people had lived near one another, the seeds and game would soon have been used up. At the same time, it was dangerous for a single family to live all alone. So the little bands formed, and the people in them intermarried. After many centuries, all the people in a given group could trace their descent back to the same Old Grandmother.

When the campers had extra food, they saved it to use in times when hunting was poor or in winter when there were no seeds to gather. Perhaps, like other early peoples, the Anasazi wrapped their surplus foods in the skins of animals and hung the bundles in trees. The Indians knew the extra supplies would be used up before the food spoiled.

The Anasazi were naturally religious, as are all peoples who live in the lap of the earth. They believed in mountain and tree and sky and rain spirits. They believed that animals and human beings had spirits, or souls, and when bodies died the spirits that had inhabited them lived on. The Indians' belief was so strong that they looked on every shelter as a temple and the head of each family as a priest. They sang and prayed to the nature spirits before they went hunting when they

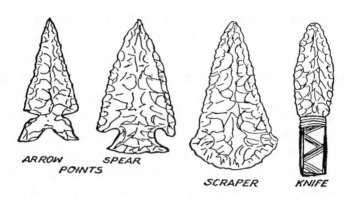

ARROW POINTS   SPEAR   SCRAPER   KNIFE

started out to search for plants to eat. And the people prayed and sang again in thanksgiving when their quest for food was successful.

Between A.D. 300 and 500 a great change took place in the lives of the Anasazi. Somehow, from somewhere, they learned about corn. They learned to plant it, to care for it while it grew, and to harvest and store it. Now that they did not have to spend so much time looking for wild foods, the Anasazi began to improve their houses, and they chose new sites for building.

With their stone axes, the Indians cut down saplings and young trees and trimmed off their branches. They used larger pieces of wood, and consequently their shelters were sturdier and larger. The Indians' cornfields were often planted along the small streams in the canyons, and the houses were built between the fields and the canyon walls. The loose, weathered stones and the soil that had eroded from the cliff faces above made it easy for the Indians to level the ground and build their houses.

Later the Anasazi began to build houses inside the caves in the bluffs. These caves were so large that several families at a time could construct brush shelters inside one of them. The cave houses were protected from the winter winds and at the same time open to the winter sun. Behind the houses were storage pits, holes scraped in the earth of the cave floors.

On the slopes in front of the caves there was plenty of room for the children to play and for their mothers and fathers to work.

Whether the Indians lived on the slopes before the caves or inside the caves themselves, they had to choose places that were near water. Although the climate of the southwestern states is generally dry, there are springs through the mountains of the Four Corners. The springs feed small streams and rivers that flow through the canyons. In winter, snow falls on the high peaks, and during the warm spring and summer months it melts and runs down the slopes. Usually there are heavy, late summer rains in the Four Corners, and when the big rains, or, as the Indians say, the Man Rains, fall there are sometimes floods in the canyons and along the dry riverbeds on the mesas.

Since the Anasazi needed water for drinking and cooking like everybody else, and since they also needed it for washing and building and farming, they had to choose building sites where they could be sure of a water supply. Even then, the Indians were always afraid of drought. Their songs and prayers spoke of their need of rain and snow. Their most important religious ceremonies were prayer dances meant to bring moisture from the sky. If there had not been a fairly good water supply in the Four Corners in the first place, the Anasazi would probably have gone on and settled somewhere else. If the rains had come in June, when the corn was ripening, instead of late August, after it was harvested, the Anasazi could not have

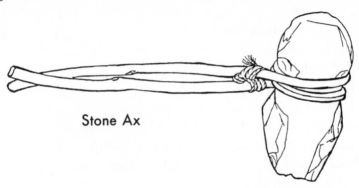

Stone Ax

developed agriculture. Then they would have lived very differently, for the other important things in their lives came because the Indians were farmers.

In good years, when there was plenty of snow and rain, the corn crops were so abundant that the Anasazi had a real storage problem. The Indians had more food than they could use, and they wanted to save it, for they knew that a bad year might come at any time. Skin bags hung in trees were unsatisfactory, and holes in caves were not much better. Rats and field mice could get at the grain and spoil it and waste it.

So the Anasazi began to line their storage pits with slabs of stone. Sometimes the builders fitted the stones together inside the holes and left them leaning against one another. Sometimes, after the slabs were set in place, the masons filled the spaces with mud. They used adobe (a-DOUGH-bee), a dense, heavy clay that occurs in many places in the Southwest. When adobe dries, it sets like cement, and it held the stone slabs in place against the walls of the storage pits.

Often the Indians filled their storage pits with corn and wild seeds, and then laid flat stone lids over the food. Sometimes an Anasazi woman plastered over her storage box with adobe mud and then forgot where she had put the food. Once in a while when an ancient Anasazi food cache is opened an archeologist finds corn and seeds that are still good to eat and will grow if they are planted.

The Anasazi had always believed that wild plants had spirits. They believed that corn, which was a better food than any wild plant, was sacred. The Indians thought that corn itself was a spirit. And they knew that before corn could grow, and its spirit come to life above the ground, it had to be planted.

The Indians began to think of the caves where the corn was stored as sacred. Soon the people began to bury their dead in the loose ground of the slopes before the caves, or to dig storage holes in the cave floors for the bodies of people they had loved. Perhaps the Indians thought the spirits of the dead would rise and grow again above the earth, as the spirit of the corn did.

When the Anasazi buried people they loved, they usually buried their possessions with them. They wrapped the body in the clothes the person used to wear. They killed the person's pet dog and wrapped its body, too, in blankets. They gave a man his weapons and his tools to take with him to the afterworld. They gave a woman her clothing and jewelry and utensils. And they gave a child its cradle and its toys. The Anasazi believed that the spirits of the material things went with the spirits of their owners to some life beyond that of the earth.

After the Anasazi learned how to raise corn, the people began to live in larger groups. Planting and harvesting gave everybody more and better food than hunting and gathering had provided. Real little towns began to form along the creeks and in the canyons. People came together from several scattered settlements to form a larger community. The former families became what we call clans, and in time the Indians made a rule requiring members of one clan to marry members of a different one.

There were no separate buildings for places of worship. People gathered in their own homes or those of their relatives to pray and sing, as they had always done. If they had noticed that a man brought home more game, or his corn grew better, when they had sung a certain song and repeated a certain prayer together, the people kept on using that combination. A man whose songs and prayers were unusually successful prayed and sang for other members of his family and for his friends. He taught his little simple ceremonies to the children as they grew up, so that they might have the same success in life as their forefathers.

The Anasazi continued to experiment with their houses for about five hundred years. They tried building brush houses out in the open again. This time, the Indians made their storage pits in the house floors and laid smooth adobe mud over the whole floor area. In order to know where the food was hidden, the Anasazi piled stones over the pit openings and then covered the stones with adobe plaster. This meant that the floor was spotted with low domes, and probably it also meant that getting around the house was pretty complicated.

The next Anasazi experiment with house-building was more complex. In A.D. 500 to 700 the Indians began to build pit houses. They used their garden hoes and digging-sticks, probably, to make holes in the ground that were four or five feet deep and sometimes as wide as twelve feet across. The holes were covered with branches, and small brush and earth were heaped over these beams to make roofs.

At first the pit houses were round or oval in shape, with sloping tunnel entrances, a little like those of Eskimo igloos. Later, the houses were rectangular, and were built with hatchways in their roofs and ladders for the people to climb in and out.

The first ladders the Anasazi used were tree trunks, with the branches broken off a few inches from the trunks. Perhaps they were trees that had been cut down to get branches to make the roofs. The stubs of the branches were used as steps. Later, the Indians made ladders by tying branches across the uprights for steps. Ladders were also made by notching poles. The Indians rested their toes against the flat side of the cut wood. And still later the ladders were made by joining two upright poles with the crosspieces and lashing the parts together with rawhide strips.

During pit house times the Anasazi built fires inside their houses for the first time. Before then, the Indians had cooked outdoors, and their houses had neither light nor heat. But now the door in the roof could be used as a chimney, with the fire built on the floor to one side of the entry hole. A stone slab was set in the floor at one side of the firepit, behind the ladder, and there was a small opening in the roof or wall opposite the slab. A current of air passed through the hole and across the fire, carrying the smoke with it. When the breeze struck the stone, it was deflected, or turned, and went upward. The smoke went out of the chimney hole, but if rain came in through the same hole, it struck the floor of the house and not the fire. The fire burned even in the worst weather.

The pit houses were real permanent homes. They had built-in furniture. The Anasazi constructed benches around the walls of the houses to use as beds by night and chairs by day. The benches could not have been too comfortable, for they were only about eighteen inches off the ground and a foot or so wide, but they were better than anything the Indians had known about before. The pit houses had good floors, of stone slabs or smooth adobe, with rectangular storage pits built into

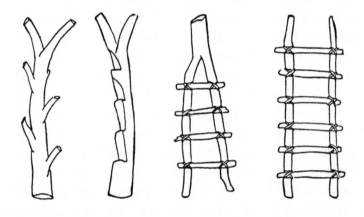

them. One part of the house, usually the space between the fireplace and the wall, was set aside as a place of worship. Here the sacred things the family owned and guarded were stored.

Some pit houses were built inside caves; others were built on the tops of mesas. The Anasazi raised several different kinds of corn by this time, and they were beginning to grow beans and squash and cotton as well. The Indians lived in real towns, with their houses grouped close together. Around each cluster of houses was a ring of storehouses, or granaries, built of poles set close together in the ground and plastered over with adobe.

Outside the circle of granaries lay the gardens and fields of the people of the community. If the pit house town were built inside a cave, the houses stood near the opening, and the granaries were built behind them, near the cave wall, where they were protected from bad weather. The cornfields were at the foot of the cliff, in the open land near the canyon walls.

Whether the people lived in the open or inside the caves, at this time they usually used the caves as cemeteries. The bodies were buried in the cave floors, behind the granaries.

Still the Anasazi went on experimenting with architecture. Perhaps the next change in house fashions came because the women, who spent more time at home than the men did, got tired of life underground. At any rate, the Indians left their pit houses and began to build above ground in the open again.

This time the Anasazi seem to have modeled their houses on their former granaries. The Indians set poles upright in the ground to form walls. Then they wove willow or spruce branches back and forth across the uprights, to fill in the spaces between them. For a while after that, the Indians lived in these open houses. Later on, the Anasazi covered their beautiful basketry walls with adobe plaster, inside and out. They laid poles across their rooms to make ceilings and filled in between the large beams with smaller trees and branches. The builders piled earth on the roofs and tramped it down till it was smooth and hard and weatherproof. After a while the Anasazi tried setting stones into the adobe plaster that covered the outer walls of the houses. The walls were stronger and harder with the stone reinforcements, and the houses lasted longer and were warmer in winter than before. So we know that the last stage in Anasazi architecture came when the Indians began to build their houses of stones carefully fitted together and held in place with adobe mortar.

Naturally, all this complicated building meant that there was a lot of work to do before construction could be started. In some places there were supplies of building stones or beds of adobe within easy reach. In other places the people had trouble finding the right materials. In that case the Indians either moved to new locations where they could get what they needed without too much trouble, or they made long trips on foot to the quarries and earth pits and brought supplies home on their backs.

Women carried the water to make the mortar. At first they used specially designed waterproof baskets for this purpose;

later, the women had pottery jars in which to carry water. A woman could carry three gallons of water at a time, at most. That would mix enough plaster to cover about two yards of wall. So the women and girls went back and forth between the stream or spring and the site of the new house, all day long, carrying baskets or jars of water on their heads.

Until after they moved out of their pit houses, the Anasazi had had only one-room homes. When they began to build above ground again, they first constructed houses with two or three rooms. The Indians began by joining the family storehouses to the living quarters, so the women could get their food supplies easily. They did not need to go outside in bad weather or to dig up their house floors. If a daughter married and wanted to continue to live near her parents, the family built a new room for the young couple, adjoining the mother's house.

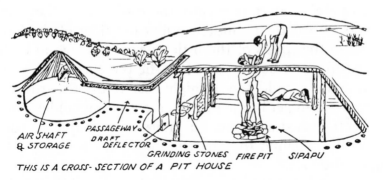

AIR SHAFT
& STORAGE
PASSAGEWAY
DRAFT
DEFLECTOR
GRINDING STONES   FIRE PIT   SIPAPU
THIS IS A CROSS-SECTION OF A PIT HOUSE

The Anasazi did not stop with joining all the rooms of one house together. They connected the houses themselves so that they made a wall of buildings around an open space, or plaza. Each house had its own door into the open area, and each house was separated from its neighbor by a solid wall.

These houses were rather dark and poorly ventilated. The people lived outdoors as much as they could and went inside to sleep or find protection from bad weather. The women worked just outside their doors on sunny days, where they could visit with their neighbors and watch their children play.

Some villages were built around the old pit houses the

people had once lived in. Instead of filling in the holes, the Indians used them as storage places for sacred articles. Perhaps the Anasazi felt that it was wrong to live and worship in the same place, and that the nature spirits and the spirits of the dead ancestors would like to have a special place of their own to live. The hole in the floor where the deflector stone was set, which was called the sipapu (SEE-pah-poo), came to be regarded as the door to the underworld where the spirits lived. The pit houses had already had storage places for sacred things, and the dead ancestors had lived in the pit houses when they were alive. The Indians were beginning to have real places of worship, although they always continued to hold family prayers and ceremonies. Archeologists call the underground temples by their Hopi name, kivas (KEE-vahs).

Now the spirits of the dead became more important than their bodies in the minds of the living people. Still, the Anasazi were careful to bury reverently those who died. Sometimes parents buried their children under the floor of the family home, so the spirits of the little ones would stay near their own people and be comforted by the presence of those who loved them. A child's spirit might even return to earth in the body of a younger brother or sister. Sometimes older people, too, were buried at home, but more often they were laid in a cave floor behind the granaries, or in the soft earth slope before the cave.

Songs and prayers were still made about hunting and planting and harvesting. But now there began to be songs and prayers and ceremonies about houses and house-building and home life as well. The Anasazi had become a settled people, and their religion had settled and taken form just as their buildings had.

The Anasazi built massive structures on the tops of mesas, along the canyon bottoms, and inside the great open caves of their country. The stone walls of these buildings were as much as five feet thick, and the stones in the walls were sometimes held in place by their own weight, without mortar. Rooms were built adjoining one another, and one above another. There were round towers and square towers. There were round kivas and square kivas. The open spaces inside the town walls were round or square, oblong or oval. Sometimes the ancient Indians seem to have built for the fun of building, not because they needed living space, for we find rooms in the ruins of the apartment-house cities that show no traces of having been occupied. Once in a while we find a room that was built without doors, and that may not have been entered since it was built. No one knows why these rooms were built.

Some houses had doors in their walls; others had doors in their roofs and had to be entered through hatchways, like the old pit houses. Still other houses had doors that were T-shaped, with the beginnings of windows on either side of a central opening. Later, real windows were built high in the walls of the outer rooms and closed with sheets of mica.

The walls of the houses in the great Indian towns were plastered with adobe, inside and out. Sometimes the plaster was smoothed and left plain; at other times designs were worked into it with the palms and outstretched fingers of the plasterers' hands. Frequently red or yellow plaster was spread on the lower part of a wall, with white or gray above it like a frieze. Occasionally the walls of the rooms were painted with geometric designs or with figures of legendary creatures.

The roofs of the houses were still made by laying beams across from wall to wall. Sometimes small branches were laid above the heavy beams in a herringbone or checkerboard pattern, before the brush and mud were heaped on to finish the roof.

Many of these later Anasazi houses had built-in bench beds along their walls. In a few houses, the Indians built low walls into the rooms from the doorways to enclose their cooking fires and channel the smoke outward. Old-fashioned families continued to use old-fashioned fires, built in holes in the floor. The southwestern Indians knew nothing about European-style chimneys until after the Spaniards came into their country. Even after the Indian men had learned to build chimneys, many families cooked outdoors except in rainy or snowy weather.

The woman of an Anasazi family had a real kitchen in which to cook. She used the space just inside the door and built her fire on one side of the opening, so the smoke could go out easily. There was a hearth of flat stones around the fireplace to protect the floor from hopping sparks and to put food that was to be kept warm.

Inside the door on the other side, the Anasazi cook kept her water supply. In the early days, the women stored their water in special cone-shaped baskets, which fitted into holes in the floor. Later on, the women made pottery jars large enough to hold several gallons of water at a time and kept them filled for household use. These big water jars were slightly porous, so the water in them was cooled by evaporation.

At the back of the room, facing toward the door, were the grinding stones, or metates (may-TAH-tays) on which the women made the cornmeal that was the Anasazi's bread. The stones were set in slab-faced boxes built into the floor and were used every day. There were jars of whole corn and of cornmeal between the metates and the fireplace, and other jars of beans and dried squash were on the opposite side of the room. Strings of dried meat and sacks of dried nuts and fruits hung from the ceiling, within easy reach. The jars and wooden spoons for cooking and the ladles for serving were stacked near the fireplace, with the bowls from which the family ate their meals.

The floors of some Anasazi houses were made by mixing adobe with deer's blood and pounding the compound smooth. When these floors dried and hardened, they were as firm as tile and were a beautiful dark red color. But deer's blood was hard to get, so most families had plain earthen floors.

Even though the Anasazi spent so much time and thought on their houses, the Indians continued to live outdoors most of the time. People who lived on the ground floor of an apartment house used the space outside their doors as an extra living room. People who lived on the upper floors used the roofs of the houses below them as places for work and visiting.

As time went on, the people of the Four Corners ornamented

their kivas more and more elaborately. Often they painted the walls of their pit house churches with wonderful murals. When the Indians wanted to change these pictures, they whitewashed over them and then painted new designs on the clean, bare walls. In one underground temple, at the old Hopi town Awatobi, archeologists found seventeen layers of paintings on the walls. In some cases, these paintings showed a great many of the ways in which the Indians did things, as well as their customs of worshiping.

During the centuries it took to learn how to build houses and cities, the Anasazi invented and used many different tools. They learned to make stone axes and bone hoes, and they soon learned how to improve each tool that was invented. The Indians made what is called a percussion ax, that is, an ax too big to lift for chopping. The percussion ax had to be swung against a tree, and its weight and the force of the blows eventually knocked the tree down. Then the butt of the log was shaped, and the branches were trimmed off with smaller hand axes.

Clever as they were, the Anasazi never learned to make rollers or wheels. When the Indians wanted to move a log or a big piece of stone, they had to tie ropes around it and drag it. And, although there were metal deposits in their country, the Anasazi never learned to make metal tools. They always depended on stone as material for implements and weapons.

When the Spaniards came to the Southwest, in 1540, they found the Anasazi living in their great apartment-house cities, surrounded by rich farms. The Spaniards called the Indian towns *pueblos,* which is the Spanish word for town, and that is the name most people give to the town-living Indians of today.

All through their history, the Anasazi loved their homes, and home is still the most important thing in the lives of Pueblo Indians. If they are taken away from their homes, even for a little while, the Indians are happy. Then they make and sing little sorrowful songs like this:

Use of Percussion Ax

THAT MOUNTAIN FAR AWAY

My home over there, my home over there,
My home over there, now I remember it!
And when I see that mountain far away,
Why, then, I weep. Alas, what can I do?
What can I do? Alas! What can I do?
My home over there, now I remember it.

Some of the greatest Indian ceremonies, like the midwinter Shalako (shah-LAH-ko) dance at Zuni Pueblo, are held to bless the houses. The spirits are invited to enter new homes, or new rooms that have been added to old houses, and to see that they are well built and that the people who live in them are happy. The Shalako ceremony lasts four days and nights, but in other pueblos the ceremonies are not so long or so elaborate. Still, most modern Indians would feel that their houses were unfinished if the spirits had not visited and blessed them.

HUNTING AND
WEAPON-MAKING

T HE ANASAZI always took their hunting seriously. For many generations, it was the only way they could get meat, or skins to make clothing. If a man were a poor hunter and did not bring in enough game for his family, they were all hungry and cold.

The Four Corners Area was never a very good place for hunting. There was some game in the canyons and on the mesas, and the Indians got all they could. But often they had to be satisfied with very little meat, or go without it entirely.

There were white-tail and mule deer, and mountain sheep and elk in the high mountains, and antelope on the plains to the east of the Four Corners country. Still farther to the east, in the true Great Plains, there were bison, or American buffalo. There may have been mountain buffalo in the ranges south and west of the Anasazi territory. Also, there were brown and cinnamon bears all through the mountains.

While there were all these different kinds of game in the Four Corners Area, there weren't many animals of any one kind. Fortunately, the Anasazi found plenty of small game in the open valleys and on the mesa tops. In the early days the Anasazi weapons were simple, and the Indians hunted small game more successfully than the larger animals.

So for a long time the Anasazi hunters concentrated on jack rabbits and cottontails in the open meadows, and snowshoe rabbits in the high mountains. The men brought home prairie dogs, chipmunks, and ground squirrels, for these small rodents were abundant and easy to catch. When the men were very lucky, they got wild turkeys, sage hens, or prairie chickens. There were trout in some of the mountain streams, but as far as we know the Anasazi never ate fish.

Just as house-building and house forms changed every time an Anasazi invented a new tool, hunting changed whenever someone learned about or invented a new weapon. The earliest hunters brought short spears, or darts, with them when they traveled southward from Alaska. These weapons had stone blades about four inches long and shafts between five and six feet in length. The lower end of the shaft, where the blade was attached, had a socket, into which the long dart shaft was fitted. When the dart struck an animal, the foreshaft was fastened into it by the blade. The true shaft dropped off, and the hunter could pick it up and use it again. He might lose the harpoonlike foreshaft, which was fairly easy to make, but he did not mind that as much as losing the laboriously polished handle on which he might have worked for months.

Even with the harpoon heads, the darts alone were not very effective. Some hunters increased their range by feathering their shafts, as arrows are feathered, with the heavy wing feathers of hawks and eagles. This helped to increase distance and improve aim, but it still did not make the weapons as efficient as the hunters wanted them to be.

The Anasazi also improved their darts by using spear throwers, or atlatls. (That is an Aztec Indian word, from Mexico, and is pronounced just the way it is spelled, AT-ul-at-ul.) An atlatl is really an arm extender. It is a flat, polished piece of wood, narrow oblong in shape, with a groove down the middle and a stop on the end of the groove. On either side of the atlatl there is a rawhide loop. An Anasazi hunter held his hand up near his shoulder, with his palm flat and his fingers turned back toward his shoulder. He held the atlatl

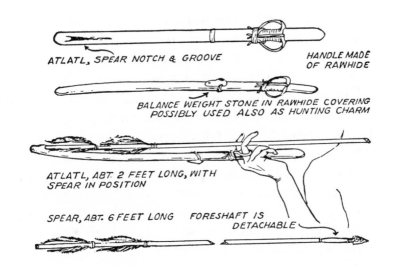

ATLATL, SPEAR NOTCH & GROOVE

HANDLE MADE
OF RAWHIDE

BALANCE WEIGHT STONE IN RAWHIDE COVERING
POSSIBLY USED ALSO AS HUNTING CHARM

ATLATL, ABT. 2 FEET LONG, WITH
SPEAR IN POSITION

SPEAR, ABT. 6 FEET LONG   FORESHAFT IS
DETACHABLE

with his forefinger and middle finger crooked through the rawhide loops. His dart rested in the groove and was held in place by the stop. The hunter threw the dart by jerking his hand forward. The dart flew ahead at the target, but the atlatl stayed in the hunter's hand. When an atlatl was used, a dart traveled farther, straighter, and harder than when it was thrown by hand.

Archeologists are still trying to find out when and where the atlatl was invented. At present they think it may have been known before the first emigrants left Asia, and that knowledge of the atlatl may have been brought across to the New World at the beginning of Indian time. We do know that it took a lot of intelligence to make such an efficient hunting tool.

At the same time that they learned to make atlatls, or maybe even earlier, the Indians learned to use string nets in hunting. The atlatls made it possible for the hunters to bring down large game animals, and the nets made it possible for the men to get a lot of small game at one time. A group of hunters held a net across the open end of a small box canyon, while another party of men came down the canyon toward them, pounding the ground and beating the bushes on either side of them with long sticks. The noise and excitement drove the rabbits and other small game into the net. The hunters closed their net on their catch as fishermen do. By this method, the Indians secured a large amount of meat in a short time. The Indians hunted in this way at the time recorded history began in Europe, about 4000 B.C. or earlier.

From the very earliest North American times, the Indians knew how to chip stones to make knives and spear points. They also knew that some stones chip off more evenly and regularly than others and that some stones cannot be chipped at all. The Indians used flint, chert, and quartz, besides obsidian, or volcanic glass, and they also used some valuable stones like crystal and agate, for weapon-making.

When he wanted to make a weapon, an Indian man went out and got a supply of good chipping stone. Perhaps he knew before he left home where there was a formation of the right kind of rock. Perhaps he had to hunt a long time to find the kind he needed. Probably men told their relatives or friends about good places to get stone, if they discovered such locations. Some deposits of stone were famous, and weapon-makers traveled long distances to reach them. Then they carried supplies of stone home with them.

The worker first broke off a piece of stone about the size of his fist. He studied this carefully, to find the grain of the stone so he could break smooth, even flakes from the core. He tied a piece of rawhide over the palm of his right hand and held the stone in his left. Then he took a pointed piece of deer's antler or wood and pressed it on a fracture line. He bore down against the point with his right palm against the upper end of the pressure point, so his weight broke the stone at the place he had chosen.

Sometimes the stoneworkers broke off several pieces at one time, and sometimes they took only one flake and saved the core to use again later. They worked the flakes down by the same pressure method, peeling off a piece at a time until the point was the right shape. Then with a smaller wood or horn tool the workers sharpened the edges of their blades

ZUNI HUNTING CHARM MADE OF AGATE, SHELL, TURQUOISE AND JET, AND TIED WITH SINEW

by taking off tiny, sharp fragments. It sounds like a slow process, but actually a skilled worker could make a stone point in a few minutes.

Among the things that the Anasazi buried with their dead were stoneworking tools and supplies of cores, as well as finished blades. Even the rawhide palm-protectors were buried with the men who had used them.

Most Anasazi hunters had small stone charms, or amulets, representing the animals they had most success hunting. The little figures were made of agate, jet, quartz, or crystal and were decorated with tiny shells or with other precious stones. The little fetishes, as luck pieces are sometimes called, were tied on atlatls or bows or on the ends of nets. Often a man wore his hunting fetish in a tiny buckskin bag around his neck.

About the time they began to build pit houses, the Anasazi started to use bows and arrows. Archeologists say that at this date some new settlers came into the Anasazi country and brought bows and arrows with them. The bows were rather short and were made of mountain mahogany or juniper wood, with strings made of yucca fibers or animal sinews. Sometimes the bows were reinforced with flat strips of sinew or mountain sheep horn glued to their backs. Reinforced bows were much more powerful than the plain wooden ones.

Indians everywhere in the New World used sinew for many purposes. It is the heavy, flat, back tendon of an animal.

When the Indians killed a large game animal, they were careful to take the sinew out whole, in two big slabs. They scraped it clean and dried it in the sun. Then they split off the tendon fibers, one or more at a time, as needed. A single sinew fiber was fine enough to sew with and strong enough to stitch pieces of buckskin together. Fibers could be twisted to make strong ropes or strings, or laid flat on pieces of wood for bow backings. Like all tendons, sinews contain glue. If the dried fibers are moistened, they will stick to each other or to other surfaces to which they are applied. So deer and mountain sheep sinew supplied the Anasazi with heavy twine and glue at the same time. It was Indian Scotch tape.

The Anasazi used sinew to fasten points and feathers to their arrows, and to attach blades to their darts. When the arrow point was made of stone, the lower end of the wooden shaft, or stave, had to be split open very carefully. The weaponmaker slipped the stone head into the opening, and then wrapped damp sinew tight and smooth around it. When the sinew dried, it shrank a little and held the point in place. The Anasazi put the stone points on their darts in the same way.

Fastening the feathers to an arrow or dart shaft was a more difficult process. The Anasazi preferred hawk feathers to all others, but some men used eagle feathers, and a few put owl-feather vanes on their arrows. They split each feather in half along its quill. Then the arrowsmiths, or fletchers, tied

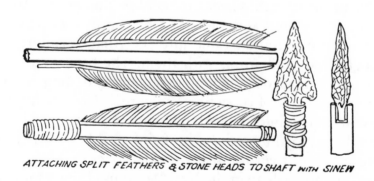

ATTACHING SPLIT FEATHERS & STONE HEADS TO SHAFT WITH SINEW

three or four feather sections in place, flat against the stave. Sometimes a man painted stripes or spots on his arrows, so he could recognize them easily.

Sometimes birds were shot for their feathers, but more often they were trapped. Certain men were particularly skillful at this kind of hunting. A trapper selected a place high on a mesa or a mountainside, away from houses and cornfields. He dug a pit large enough to hide in, and covered it with brush and leaves. He spread a net over the branches and hid it with leaves and grass. Then he tied a rabbit or a small bird to one of the branches and hid inside the pit. When an eagle or hawk stooped to the prey, the hunter seized its legs from inside the trap and then tied the bird. Caged hawks and eagles were kept in many pueblos, on the rooftops; the birds' feathers were used to fletch weapons and were also used in making ceremonial objects.

The Anasazi made songs and prayers about all their tasks, and their descendants sing many of the same songs today. Perhaps a craftsman's song would go like this:

SONG OF THE ARROW MAKER

Blue flint from the east,
See, I have it.
Yellow stone from the south,
See, I have it.
Black obsidian from the west,
See, I have it.
White quartz from the north,
See, I have it, too.
Oh, my colored arrows,
You will be beautiful.
You will fly beautifully
On hawk feathers.

On eagle feathers you will fly.
You will bring food,
Food for all the people,
My colored arrows.

And probably the arrowmaker kept time to the song with his work, tapping along as his horn point struck against the stone. He believed that singing made his work easier and made what he worked on better.

The Anasazi arrowmakers were not hunters; they were usually older men. The hunters were young men who were strong enough to travel long distances on foot to find large game and to carry the meat back when they had killed it.

Because large game was rather scarce, the hunters had a great responsibility. They kept themselves in training, like athletes. The hunters ate special foods at special times. They lived away from their families and slept in the kivas for four nights before each hunting trip. They got up early in the morning, and besides doing their shares of the other work, they ran long distances at dawn.

During the four days a hunter spent preparing to go out into the mountains, he prayed and sang a great deal. He talked to the animal spirits. He explained to them that he was going to kill the living animals, not because he wanted to but because the people needed meat and skins. He asked the spirits to help him, and to send him the kind of animal the people needed.

The hunter left his village during the fourth night. He went through the high trees, up the mountainside, with four arrows in a case on his back, and his bow in a separate bag tied beside the quiver. When the hunter saw his game, he prayed once more while he strung his bow and fitted the arrow to the string, to ask the animal to forgive him for killing it. Then he loosed his arrow.

Often the hunter brought down the game at his first shot. If he lost all four arrows, he turned around and went home.

He believed the animal spirits were angry with him, or that he had not prayed and sung in the right way, or that for some other reason he was not meant to bring meat home at that time. Then he waited, sometimes for several months, before he went hunting again.

The Anasazi hunting songs are very sacred, and so we do not know what they are like. That is why there is no large-game song here to show you the words to those songs.

The modern Pueblo Indians still hunt game as their ancestors did, by netting rabbits and other small rodents. At Jemez Pueblo, near Albuquerque, New Mexico, everybody in town goes rabbit hunting once or twice a year. The people get up very early in the morning, before daylight. They dress and eat breakfast by lantern light. Then they gather together lunches and pick up long willow switches, ready to start when the time comes.

Before sunrise, a messenger calls to the people to come out of their houses. Quietly, without any unnecessary talking, the people leave their town and go out on a mesa to the north. There the women and the old men and young boys and girls make a great circle, almost a mile across. In the dusk of the coming morning the people stand still, waiting. They are spread out so they can hardly see the shapes of the people to the left and right of them.

Inside the first circle is a second smaller one, made up of the men and boys, standing almost shoulder to shoulder. The outer ring of people faces inward; the inner circle faces outward, as if the groups were choosing partners for a dance. When the hunting priest gives the signal, the people in the outside ring begin to move toward the center, closing in and drawing nearer to one another as they go. And as they go, the people sweep their switches across the grass and weeds and pound them on the ground. They stamp their feet and shout and sing, but the men in the inner circle stand waiting quietly.

As the outer circle closes, birds and animals are driven toward the circle of men and boys. The hunters strike the game with bent wooden clubs, called rabbit sticks. Sometimes they throw the rabbit sticks, instead of striking with them. Because they are flat on one side and are slightly angled in the center, rabbit sticks can be thrown on a curve, like boomerangs.

When the circles meet, the community hunt is ended. The people gather up their game and take it back to the pueblo. Then the hunting priest divides it. He gives each family meat to eat at once, and more meat to dry and prepare for winter use. He tells each woman to bring a share of the dried meat back to him. He will put it in the community storehouse, to give to people who need it or to distribute to everybody in a time of famine.

Here is a hunting song like the ones the women sing when they are waiting for a rabbit hunt to start:

WOMEN'S HUNTING SONG

See, we are standing waiting.
See, waiting we stand.
Our father, the sun,
We wait for you. We wait for your light.
Now come up. Rise over the mountains.
Give us your light.
Bless our hunt with your light,
Our father the sun,
See, we are standing waiting.
See, waiting we stand.

That is a very quiet song, and the Indian women would almost whisper it, for fear of frightening the game away and making their children go hungry in winter. Probably the earliest Anasazi women sang the same kind of little songs when they went out to help their men with net hunting.

Usually the Anasazi were peaceful people; in fact, the name

Rabbit Hunt at Jemez Today

of the Hopi means "The Peaceful Ones." House-building and farming kept the people too busy to go out and make war on other Indian groups. Sometimes the Indians of the towns were attacked, and when that happened the Anasazi fought to protect their families and their homes.

The Anasazi used the same weapons in fighting that they did in hunting. If they were forced to, the men probably fought with their digging sticks and hoes, as well as with their bows and arrows and darts. They had no reason to invent special weapons for killing other people.

GARDENS GROW
INTO FARMS

ALL SEED-GATHERING peoples, everywhere, have about the same tools and implements for getting their food. In the earliest times the Anasazi were no different from all others.

Seed gatherers were usually women. They started out with their bare hands and pulled up roots with their fingers and scooped seeds into their palms. When someone had a handful of seeds, she ate them, or immediately gave them to her husband or children. When she and her family got hungry again, this very early woman went out to gather more seeds or roots.

After a time, and probably it was a very long time, some Indian genius picked up a stick and began digging with it. After she had thrust one end of the stick into the ground again and again, she noticed that it was slightly sharpened and pointed, and that it went into the ground more easily. So the same wise Indian, or one of her great-grandchildren, began sharpening and hardening her digging sticks by thrusting one end into the fire and then grinding it, end down, against the ground or a stone until it had a good, lasting point.

As long as the Anasazi lived on wild roots and seeds, a fire-sharpened digging stick was a satisfactory tool. Nobody dug much at a time, and when a digger got tired she could stop and rest.

The women made bags by turning the skins of rabbits or ground squirrels inside out. They sewed up the eyeholes and other openings besides the mouth, and put their extra seeds in the bags. Sometimes a woman was lucky enough to marry a good hunter, and she had buckskin seed bags.

When the Anasazi began to make and use baskets, about A.D. 11 to 100, seed-gathering tools improved considerably. The women made basketry scoops, shaped rather like curved tennis rackets, to knock seeds from the wild grasses and weeds. The women also had large and small carrying baskets. As they walked through the high grasses in seed-harvesting time, or went along the vines where wild berries grew, the women knocked the ripe seeds and fruits down into their gathering baskets with their scoops. When a woman had filled her small hand basket, she emptied it into the big cone-shaped basket she carried between her shoulders. In order to keep her hands and arms free to work, the woman suspended the carrying basket from her head by means of a strap across her forehead. A carrying cord that is worn about the head is called a tumpline. The big carrying baskets held two or three bushels of seeds at a time, and the women had to walk bent far forward, and move slowly, in order to balance the loads on their backs.

In the fall the women and children gathered piñon nuts. These are tiny, hard, dark brown nuts that are formed in the cones of scrub pines. The nuts taste good and are rich in oil, so the Anasazi valued them. When the cones ripen, they pop open, and the ground around the piñon tree is scattered with the nuts. They must be scraped together and scooped up by handfuls. The piñon trees do not bear well every year, and in good piñon years the Indians had to work fast and gather enough nuts to last through two or three poor years.

At about the same time the Anasazi began to make and use baskets, they also learned about corn. Where they heard of the grain, or how, we do not know. We do know that

Indians in Old Mexico and in Peru, far to the south of the Anasazi area, knew about corn and how to grow it before the Indians of the Four Corners country did.

Our botanists have identified the wild ancestors of wheat and rye and barley, the most important Old World food grains. Although botanists have not yet found the wild ancestor of corn, most agree that it sprang from a grass native to Mexico. Ever since the time of the first corn we know about, corn has been unable to grow without man's help. It must be planted and cared for in certain ways in order to mature. Corn cannot seed itself and produce a crop unaided. Wheat, rye, and barley can.

So we can only guess at the story of the Anasazi discovery of corn. Perhaps some of the men went south from the Four Corners on a hunting trip. They may have met other Indians, who needed meat. The Anasazi traded dried venison to the strangers, perhaps. In return, they received a new food— parched corn or cornmeal. The men from the Four Corners ate the grains and liked them. Perhaps they stayed in the south long enough to learn how corn should be planted and tended. Then the travelers returned to their homes, taking new food and new knowledge with them.

This first corn didn't look much like the roasting ears we eat. It was a wild grass with tiny ears no larger than a thumb. On these little nubbins there were kernels not much larger than grains of wheat. The very first corn was yellow and white. Later red, blue, and speckled types were introduced or developed. Popcorn was discovered by some Indian group, and many others began planting it

It is hard for any of us to imagine what a change corn made in Anasazi life. The grain wasn't easy to raise, and a lot of the tiny ears were needed to feed a family. Getting the kernels off the ears was hard work, and grinding the kernels to make cornmeal was even harder. But no matter how difficult it was to raise and harvest and store a corn crop, the life of the Indians was much easier than in the days when the Anasazi had to depend on wild seeds and fruits and nuts to supplement

Gathering Seeds in Early Anasazi Days

what meat the hunters could supply.

Everything in Anasazi life changed after the Indians had corn. If you plant a cornfield, you have to stay near it, to keep deer and rabbits from eating the plants. You must hoe and water and care for your crop all during the growing season. You can't move away whenever you feel like it, unless you are willing to lose your grain and your work.

If you know you have to stay in one place all summer, you build a real house, instead of a brush shelter, just as the Anasazi did. If you have corn, you can store food from season to season, and everybody can be better nourished all year. More babies are born and survive when their mothers have enough to eat. Old people live longer and are healthier. The population increases because people who are not able to work with their hands can still be fed. And instead of living as a family, people begin to live as members of a community— first of a village and then of a town.

When they were sure of a good supply of food, the Anasazi could give their time and attention to other parts of life besides earning their livings. In the months between the growing seasons, the men had time to work with their hands and to become fine craftsmen. They learned to carve wood and stone, to make jewelry, to weave, and to paint.

Because of the new feeling of security and leisure that came to the Indians after they began to plant gardens, they developed art and music and dancing. They told and retold their stories, and repeated and improved their poetry until they had a perfected style. Corn was not only food; it was material for thought.

All kinds of new things had to be invented because the Anasazi had corn. Pottery was one of them, but pottery is a whole chapter by itself. Right now we should concentrate on gardening and gardening tools.

In order to plant corn, the Anasazi had to clear the tall weeds from a patch of ground and loosen the earth thoroughly so that sunlight and air could penetrate the soil. They planted at least four seeds at a time in order to raise one cornstalk.

Like most gardeners, the Indians soon learned that plants were most easily cared for if they were set in rows. The cornfields were large and needed plenty of open space, so they were laid out along the streams or on the mesas, away from the houses. If a man's fields were quite a long way from home, he would build a shelter nearby and sleep there during the growing season. In later years whole families often moved into summer houses near their fields.

All the time the corn was growing, the Indians had to watch it. Weeds had to be cleared away, and the soil had to be piled up around the roots of the plants to hold the moisture in the ground. The climate is dry in the Four Corners. Every drop of

Corn Cultivation

dampness counted in raising a corn crop. When there was a spring or summer rain, the Indian farmers deepened the rows between their plants so the water drained into the little ditches. A short time before the Spanish invasion, the Anasazi learned to dig real irrigation ditches and to run the water from a creek or river onto their cornfields.

With so much cultivating to do, the Indian farmers needed better tools than digging sticks. This time we know what they invented because the implements have been found. First, an Indian farmer had a simple digging stick with one pointed end. The other end was round and useless. So the farmer whittled the round end of the stick down thin and flat like a blade. Then he had a double-ended, combination tool, with a spade at one end and a point at the other.

The Anasazi gardeners soon realized that the flat end of the tool was more useful in a cornfield than the sharp end. They began to choose pieces of wood that were naturally wider and flatter than the sticks they had used before. And then someone began to make the blade and the handle out of separate pieces of wood and tie them together with sinew. The last invention was a real hoe, with a mountain sheep's or deer's shoulder-blade bone as a blade.

The Anasazi women continued to harvest wild seeds and piñon nuts and berries, but corn cultivation was the men's work. That was probably because the women were too busy with their families and their houses to go out to work in the fields day after day. It may have been because the men had always hunted and provided the family's meat, and when corn became their most important food the Indians thought it, too, should be the men's responsibility.

Almost at the same time that the Anasazi learned about corn, they were introduced to two other cultivated plant foods, squash and beans. Like corn, these vegetables were developed in the Western Hemisphere. Both were unknown in Europe and Asia before 1492. Wherever the Indians raised gardens, they planted these three foods. Because they always went together in Indian life, corn, squash, and beans are known as the American Vegetable Triad.

In the very earliest cornfields we know anything about, the Indians planted squash vines between the clumps of corn. Probably one reason for the custom was to shade the young corn plants with the wide leaves of the squash, pumpkins, or cucumbers. The vines had plenty of ground to run over in the cornfields, and they needed the space in order to develop properly. The farmers could take care of two vegetables at once, without extra effort.

Beans do not require so much space as corn or squash to grow well, so the Anasazi planted them in smaller patches near the houses. A woman could cultivate the family's bean crop in her spare time and keep an eye on the children while she did it.

Often the first beans planted in the spring were started in the kivas. There, in the warm darkness, the seeds were spread on basketry trays and sprinkled with water. When the first green sprouts showed, the beans were carried outdoors and set in the prepared garden beds. There were bean-sprouting ceremonies and songs and prayers in many Indian towns, for bean-sprouting was a sign of spring.

Although the triad vegetables formed their most important crops, the Anasazi also raised cotton, tobacco (in about A.D. 500 at the time of the Dark Ages in Europe), and sunflowers. We know that the Indians ate the sunflower seeds, and some people think they may have raised the cotton for the oil in its seeds as well as for its fibers. The first cotton plants in North America were cultivated in Mexico. Later cotton was raised in southern Arizona, and we are fairly sure that the Anasazi learned about the plant through trading with the Indians to the south of them. Apparently the eastern Indians were the first to raise tobacco, and that plant must have traveled a long way before it found a place in the Anasazi gardens.

When the Anasazi became farmers who lived in towns and went out to work in their fields, their way of thinking about life must have changed almost as much as their way of working. Perhaps until then a man and a woman owned their house together. They spent about the same amount of time at home. They moved whenever they needed to, and whenever they moved the people built new shelters.

Now the men were gone all day during the growing seasons, besides the time that they spent hunting, and the women stayed at home by themselves. They cared for the houses and did most of their work indoors or on their doorsteps. After a while, the people began to say that the women owned the houses and the men owned the fields. When a woman died, her daughters or nieces inherited her house. When a man died, he bequeathed his fields to his sons or nephews. This was a sensible division, for it meant that both men and women owned the places they needed to earn their livings.

Today, the modern Anasazi speak of "my mother's house" and "my father's fields," and make songs about them. And the modern Indians still trace their families back through the mother's side, as the early Anasazi probably did, instead of through the father's side as we do.

The Anasazi thought the gardens and the plants that grew in the gardens were the gifts of the spirits, and had spirits of their own. The Indians had ceremonies based on raising crops, and these became the most important of the Anasazi ceremonies. They may have begun with little simple songs like this one:

PLANTING SONG

See, I am letting the seed fall on the earth.
See, I am helping the roots grow in the earth.
By and by the corn will grow tall,
It will make food for all the people,
And we will all sing and dance and be happy.

A farmer could sing that song in time to his digging, and his hoe would strike the ground like a drumstick beating on a drumhead. Or perhaps he sang in time with the movements of his hands and body as he dropped seeds on the earth.

Later the planting songs became very long, and more and more sacred, as they were handed down from father to son. Each generation added a verse or thought to the original poem. Here is a sacred corn song from Zuni Pueblo:

THE GROWTH OF THE CORN

Yonder toward the East
With prayers
We made our road go forth.
How the world will be
How the days will be
We desired to know.
Perhaps if we are lucky
Our earth mother
Will wrap herself in a fourfold robe
Of white meal,
Full of frost flowers.

Then in the spring when she is replete with living waters
All different kinds of corn
In our earth mother
We shall lay to rest.
Into their sun father's daylight
They will come out standing;
Yonder to all the directions
They will stretch forth their hands calling for rain.
Then with their fresh waters
The rain makers will pass us on our roads.

Thus we shall always live

That yonder to where the life-giving road of your
*   sun father comes*
Your roads may reach.
That you may finish your roads;

For this I add to your breath.
To this end, my fathers,
My children,
May all of you be blessed with light.

When the Spaniards arrived in the Southwest, they taught the Indians many things. The Anasazi learned how to plow their lands and to plant wheat, rye, and barley; how to raise fruit trees and berry vines; how to cultivate garlic, onions, chile peppers, and many other vegetables.

But the Spaniards also learned a great deal from the Indians. The newcomers found out about corn and beans and squash and tobacco for the first time, and they took the Indian plants back to Europe with them. We hear so often about the things the Indians learned from the Spaniards that sometimes we forget about the parts of our everyday lives that the colonists learned from the Indians.

BASKETS, BASKET-MAKING, AND BASKETMAKERS

NOBODY KNOWS when or where the first baskets were invented. Baskets are made all over the world by many different peoples. They may be simple containers, decorated only with the natural tones of the plants from which they are made. Or baskets may be extremely complicated and decorated with woven designs, dyes, paints, or embroidery.

Usually one of the strands of which a basket is made is called an *element*. If the basket is plaited, its heavy, supporting elements are called *warps,* and the lighter elements crossing the warps are called *wefts*.

Some baskets are sewed instead of plaited. In this case, the supporting element is a *coil* of grass or twigs, or a bundle or single rod of willow or redbud. The *stitching* element is a strand of grass, yucca, bark, or other material.

The Anasazi began making both plaited and sewed baskets before our knowledge of dates in the Four Corners begins. Probably basket-making started before the Indians settled down in their permanent homes. There were plenty of plants suitable for basket-making in the Four Corners Area, and the Anasazi soon learned to use all of them.

Perhaps the Indians used portable skin containers for some time after they invented basketry. But after they began to have gardens and to store food from one season to the next, the Anasazi needed larger, stronger vessels than they had for keeping wild seeds.

In their earliest house-building and farming period, the Anasazi made so many baskets, and the baskets were so fine and so interesting, that archeologists call this period the Time of the Basketmakers. The ruined houses in the Four Corners held great quantities of the baskets, many of them still whole and perfect, when the scientists dug into their floors.

Plaited baskets seem to have been made earlier than sewed ones, although it is hard to be certain which type came first. However, we can be sure that the Anasazi made a great many plaited baskets. They also made plaited cloth at an early date.

Possibly the first baskets were invented by accident. When Anasazi women were out gathering roots or seeds, they may have twisted twigs or leaves together to make holders for the food they planned to carry home. As the women went along, perhaps they noticed that some plants were easier to twist than others, and that the leaf or bark strands of the same plants held together especially well.

So perhaps the next step in basket-making came when some woman picked yucca leaves or stripped the bark off juniper roots, and saved the fibers to take home with her. The next time she wanted to go root-gathering, she twisted a container together out of the materials she had in the house and carried it with her when she left home.

After a while some woman must have realized that if she kept the leaves and bark too long, they dried out and were hard to bend and shape. And at the same time she saw that if she moistened the materials as she worked, her work was easier and the finished vessel was strong and sturdy when it dried. A basket that was well made lasted a long time, if the owner took care of it.

From then on, the women were busy all the time. Some of them may have stopped work when they had all the baskets they needed around the house, but others went on working. They made baskets for their own amusement, as women today knit or do needlepoint. Probably the women who especially liked to make baskets, and who practiced hard and grew skillful at their work, became basket-making specialists. These experts may have traded their work to their neighbors for cornmeal or dried meat, so they would have more time to give to basket-making. But every Anasazi woman must have known how to make baskets, and it was probably good pick-up work to do while they were talking or watching their children play in front of the caves in the afternoon.

As the women acquired more skill, the baskets they made became bigger and fancier. There were basketry plates and bowls and saucers. There were the special basketry water jars with cone-shaped bases we have already mentioned, which were set in the kitchen floors. There were basketry canteens, coated with piñon pitch, that the hunters and traders carried with them on their trips. There were work baskets and carrying baskets and cooking baskets. There were basketry cradles, and at one time there were basketry houses and woven mattresses.

Each plant to be used for basket-making had to be gathered at a particular time of the year. Willow bark is best in the spring, when the sap first flows into the branches, and the bark is soft and pliable and easily stripped from the branches. Later in the year the bark hardens and sticks tight to the wood, and cannot be peeled off the branches in long, even strips.

Yucca leaves are at their best in the early summer, when they grow straight and tall and supple. Afterward the leaves dry out, and are too brittle and tough to work easily. Juniper-root bark can be used in spring or summer, and the women dug for it after a rain, when the earth was moist and easy to turn.

Dye plants, too, ripen at different times. Chamisa, or rabbitbrush, which gives a beautiful yellow color, blooms in August and September. The Anasazi women gathered the blossoms and dried and saved them. Cactus fruits, which give a pink-lavender color, can be gathered in July and August. The color does not last long, but until it fades it looks very pretty on a basket.

Basketry House, about A.D. 500

Yucca is not a dye, but the leaves can be bleached or can be left pale green, which gradually fades to yellow. Devil's claw is a shiny dark brown, almost black, and was used to decorate some basketry. The natural dark red-brown of the willow bark and the red of juniper-root bark were also used to give color to Anasazi basketry. The women used red, brown, blue, yellow, and white earths, mixed with water and sinew glue, to paint colors on their baskets. Some baskets have been found with designs woven into them and other designs painted over the woven ones.

To make a plaited basket, a woman lays five long parallel elements on the ground in front of her. She interlaces them with four long crossing warps. The middle of this cross makes the small center of the bottom of the basket. This process can be continued to produce a large mat. If the warps are dampened, they can be bent upward to form the sides of the basket, and then turned back on themselves to make a plaited edge.

To continue weaving a spiral for the bottom of a basket she puts her first weft over the first warp on her right (or on the left, if she is left-handed), under the second warp, over the third, and the fourth, and over the fifth. She goes all the way around the eight crossed warps, and when she has returned to the starting point, the weft has gone up and down sixteen times. She adds a single rod to make an uneven number of warps, so her wefts will not cross her warps at the same points.

As she works, the woman pulls the weft very tight, and each pull draws the warps closer together and holds them more firmly in place. When the weft has gone around four times, the worker begins to add more warps. She puts four new elements on a radius between each two arms of the cross. We call the first set of crossed warps the *primary* warps, or *primaries*. The added warps are called the *secondaries*.

The basketmaker can add as many sets of secondaries as she needs. When the first sixteen have been fastened in place with four turns of the weft, she can insert others; and when they are secure, she can add still more. It all depends on how big she wants the basket to be.

When the woman reaches the end of her first weft strand, she starts to work with another. She does not tie the two wefts together or tie them to the warps. Instead, she leaves the ends of the wefts on the side of the basket until it is finished. Then she pulls them tight for the last time and trims the tips off with her stone knife.

To make the sides of the basket, the woman moistens the warps thoroughly and bends them upward at an angle. Then she starts a new weft just above the bend in the warps and works it in tightly. She continues around the sides of the basket, either with the simple over-and-under plaiting she has used on the bottom or with a more elaborate pattern, such as under-one-over-two, or under-one-over-three-under-two-over-three-under-three-over-three-under-two-over-three-under-one. Baskets can be plaited with checkerboard, herringbone, or diamond twills worked in with the wefts.

The worker may finish the edge of her basket in any one of several ways. She can cut off the tips of the warps and twist the last weft over-and-under the next to the last, in a sort of hem. She can add other elements to the weft and make a braided edge. Or she can bend the warps inward over the wefts and work them back under the wefts toward the center of the basket.

This kind of basket-making is called *single-weft plaiting* or *simple basket plaiting*. The Anasazi also made more complicated baskets, with two sets of wefts. Two-weft plaiting is usually called *twining*.

A twined basket starts with the same warps, laid in the same loose cross, as does a simple plaited basket. The worker starts her two wefts in the same place that she would a single one, on the right. She puts her *A* weft over the first warp, under the second, over the third, and so on, just the way the single warp went on the plaited basket. The *B* weft goes *under* the first warp, *over* the second, *under* the third, *over* the fourth, and so on, all the way around the basket. Each time the two wefts come together between two warps, the worker twists the wefts together, or *twines* them around each other. That is how this method of plaiting got its name.

The worker could add either warp or weft elements to a twined basket as she did to a simple plaited one. There probably was no advantage in having two weft elements instead of one, for single weft baskets can be just as strong as those with two wefts. Perhaps the women got tired of making one kind of plait and tried the other kind for a change.

Plaited baskets can be either soft or stiff, whichever the maker wants them to be. Plaiting can be used to make mats and bags, as well as baskets. The warp elements can be either stiff or pliable, but the wefts must be flexible, because they move while the warps stay in place.

Coiled baskets are always stiffer than plaited ones. That is because the foundation of a coiled basket is a rod or a bundle of material. In making a coiled basket, the worker starts by making a loop, as small as possible, with the foundation element. She knots her *sewing* element around the loop, to hold them both securely in place. Then she turns the loop, so the foundation makes a second coil around the first one, and sews the two loops together with the stitching element. Sometimes the worker makes a hole in the foundation element with a pointed tool, like a shoemaker's awl. She threads the sewing element through the hole and pulls it tight. Usually new sewing elements are added as they are in plaited basketry, with loose, untied ends left on the inner surface until the basket is finished. New foundation elements have their ends cut on a slant and are fitted to the slanted ends of the old ones, so the two overlap.

The stitches on a coiled basket can be spaced like the bricks in a wall, so that the stitches in the second row fit into the spaces between the stitches of the first row. Or the stitches can be placed one above another like the steps of a ladder. Or each new stitch can skip two or three old ones. Many different ways of spacing the stitches are found on coiled Anasazi baskets.

The edge of a coiled basket is made by sewing over and over, sometimes in a whip stitch and sometimes in a buttonhole

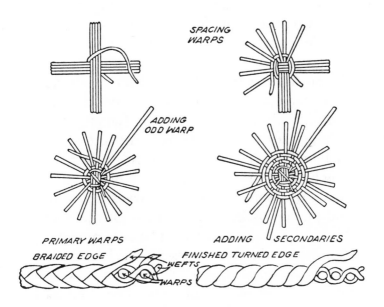

Plaited Basketry Techniques

or blanket stitch, to fasten down the coiling element.

The designs on plaited baskets are always angular, because the wefts must cross the warps at right angles. That does not mean that all plaited baskets look alike, naturally. Besides the designs that are worked into them, plaited baskets may have designs painted on them. The different weaving patterns, and differently dyed or natural-colored elements add a great deal of variety to the patterns of plaiting.

The designs on coiled baskets are also angular, because the stitches are taken at right angles to the supporting elements. If dyed sewing elements of different colors are used, human or animal figures, or geometric designs, can be stitched into the baskets.

Either plaited or sewed baskets can be made with lids and handles, and they can be large or small. These details depend on what the basket is to be used for. A storage basket, for instance, needs a lid but not a handle. A carrying basket, on the other hand, needs a handle or a fastening for a tumpline, but no lid. A basket scoop, for gathering seeds, needs a long handle, while a catch basket, into which the seeds are swept, needs a short one.

The finest Anasazi baskets, and the greatest number of them, were made before the Indians of the Four Corners invented pottery. The Indians did not forget how to make baskets, though, even after they had other utensils to replace them. At Jemez Pueblo, the women still make plaited yucca winnowing baskets, to sell to the women of the other pueblos and to tourists. In some of the Hopi towns, the women make coiled and plaited basketry bread trays for their own use, as well as for sale. They also make other baskets, modeled on their old-time storage and carrying baskets, which they sell as curios or to be used as wastebaskets. The Jemez baskets have no decoration but their twilled plaiting. The Hopi baskets are often decorated with geometric designs or with human or animal figures. These are worked out in elements dyed with vegetable colors.

We can be sure that the Anasazi women had basket-making songs. None of these songs has come down to us, but, if they were like other Indian songs, they probably went like this:

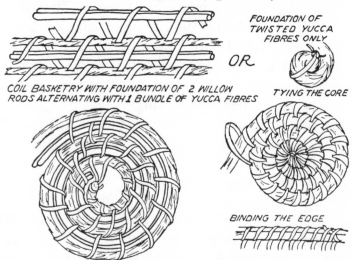

FOUNDATION OF TWISTED YUCCA FIBRES ONLY

OR

COIL BASKETRY WITH FOUNDATION OF 2 WILLOW RODS ALTERNATING WITH 1 BUNDLE OF YUCCA FIBRES

TYING THE CORE

BINDING THE EDGE

Coiled Basketry Techniques

SONG OF THE BASKETMAKER

On the flat mesas
I gathered yucca.
Along the spring-time streams,
I pulled the willow branches.
High on the mountainside
I dug for cedar roots.
Spring, summer, and fall
I looked for baskets.
Now the basket is growing under my hands,
I turn it around,
I bend the strands,
And the basket grows as the plant grew.
Leaf patterns for the yucca,
Steps like climbing branches,
Mountain forms from the cedar,
All these I put in my basket.
Then when I see it
When my children see it
When we fill it with corn for the winter,
We remember our Mother the Earth.

AT THE END OF A PIECE OF STRING

THE ASIATIC ancestors of the Anasazi probably invented string without knowing it. Someone decided that the rough bark strand he used to drag a piece of firewood would be stronger if he twisted two fibers together. As the man stood there in the woods, rolling two fragments of bark between his palms, he couldn't possibly imagine the industry he was starting.

String-making itself wasn't complicated. It was important for the Indians to find the best materials they could and to figure out the best ways of twisting the strands, but that was all. In the Four Corners, the Anasazi found a good assortment of plant fibers, for the same plants that produced the best basket-making materials also yielded the best string and ropes.

At first the Indians must have twisted their cordage between their palms or with their fingers. Working with the hands alone was awkward, and it was hard for one spinner to give the cord a twist hard enough to hold it. Two people working together could do a better job, but if you need a piece of string in a hurry you can't always find someone to help you twist it. The best way the Indians could discover to make string, and one that they used for many centuries, was to spin the cord between the palm of one hand and the bare thigh.

With the fingers of the other hand, the strand could be drawn out and twisted back as it was rolled forward against the skin of the leg.

Even before they settled in the Four Corners, the Anasazi had learned that if one string did well, two did better. They must have begun by tying two cords together, crisscross, and pulling the four ends up around whatever they wanted to carry, to make a second knot opposite the first one. Then someone tied a third string around a bundle, crossing the first two knotted strands, as we tie a string around the middle of a package we plan to mail.

When strings are knotted together at right angles, they form a loose net. Real netting began when the strings were knotted *before* they were fastened around the article the Anasazi wanted to carry. As the Indians grew more skillful, their netting became more and more complicated. The Anasazi made strings and nets from whole yucca leaves, juniper-root bark, the strong, fine, inner fibers of the yucca leaves, willow bark, animal sinews, dog hair, human hair, and cotton. The Indians also used combinations of material to make cords and strings.

One combination cord that was popular with the Anasazi in their basket-making days was made of yucca or wild hemp fiber combined with rabbit fur. When a man had saved a good supply of rabbit skins, he made this kind of string. He started by cutting each skin into a single long strip. He laid the hide out on the ground or on a flat rock and began to cut around the edge with the point of his stone knife. When he had trimmed away a strip of hide about an inch wide and a foot long, leaving it still attached to the hide, the worker pulled and stretched and straightened the piece he had cut. As he continued to cut, he continued to stretch and straighten his rabbit skin string, and then rolled it into a ball with the fur side of the strip turned out. By the time the cut reached the center of the hide, the worker had a strip of fur several feet long, rolled up and ready to use.

The worker cut up all his rabbit skins in the same way. When he had a good supply of fur strips, he prepared yucca cord.

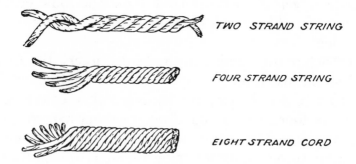

TWO STRAND STRING

FOUR STRAND STRING

EIGHT STRAND CORD

For this he used the fibers of yucca leaves, discarding the fleshy parts of the leaves. He spun the cords on his thigh and folded the twisted strings together to make hanks, rather than balls, of fibers.

Perhaps the man saved the next step in his work to do in the winter, when he had plenty of free time. Even without being interrupted by garden work and hunting, it took a skillful craftsman a long time to finish making his cord.

When the strings were ready, the worker sat down on the ground, with his legs folded under him and his feet turned to the right, if he were right-handed. (If he were left-handed, of course, he did everything in reverse.) He held the two balls of cord inside the bend of his knee, so they would not roll around and become soiled or lost. The man took an end of each cord in the fingers of his left hand and laid the strands across his right thigh. With the palm of his right hand he rolled the two strands together and away from him, while he twisted them with his left thumb and forefinger. When the string had reached his left arm's length and was too long to hold out-stretched, the worker began to roll his yucca and fur cord into a ball or wind it around a piece of wood. He laid the finished ball or spool on the ground beside him as he continued to work.

If the worker were really skillful, only the fur showed on the surface of the cord. The finished string was about an inch around, and was soft and fluffy to touch. The firm yucca string was almost hidden inside the soft fur strand.

The Anasazi and Pueblos have continued to make fur cords of this sort all through their history, and the Hopi men make them today, though this practice is declining. Between A.D. 500 and 700, when the Anasazi were living in pit house cities inside the great caves of the Four Corners, some men began to use turkey-feather cordage. You can imagine how fine and soft these cords were, and what a lot of work it was to make one of them. Nobody makes feather cordage today. The wild turkeys have been overhunted by non-Indian hunters, and tame turkeys, like chickens and ducks, do not seem to have the right kind of feathers for spinning.

When they could trade cornmeal for buffalo hair, the Anasazi made buffalo-wool yarn. Dog hair was easier to get, and they used it for belts and fine tumplines. The Indians had large, long-haired dogs, with dark-spotted white coats. By separating the light and dark hair, the spinner could make thread of two different colors. If he combined light and dark, he could spin yarn of a third shade.

Human hair cordage was an Anasazi specialty. The women let their thick hair grow as long as they could. When a woman's hair was a foot or eighteen inches long, her husband cut it off close to her head with a stone knife. He then twisted the strands of hair to make cords. In some cases the cords were braided, in others they were spun. Hair cords and ropes were extremely strong and could be used for heavy work.

Milkweed string was another Anasazi product. Very few peoples anywhere in the world have succeeded in working with milkweed down because it is so light and fluffy that it is hard to handle. At Zuni Pueblo, in the 1890s, men made milkweed cordage by first taking the seeds, with the down sticking to them, out of the pods. They laid the mass out on a bed of fine white sand on the floor of the kiva. Then, with fine, flexible forked rods they whipped the down. It would leave the seeds and cling to the sticks, and the workers stripped the fluffy white stuff off their wands and laid it aside, with all the fibers lying in the same direction, ready for spinning.

Probably the people to the south of the Anasazi country, who seem to have taught the northern Indians many important things, also taught them both planting and spinning of cotton. Native American cotton is a short-stapled variety; that is, its individual fibers are less than an inch long. They stick tight to the seeds, and the seeds stick tight to the bolls. Cleaning the cotton and preparing it for spinning are harder work than making cords from some wild plant fibers. The Zuni whipped the cotton in the same way that they whipped milkweed, and they had probably learned the process from their ancestors.

Fortunately, the Anasazi did not have to spin the wispy cotton fibers on their thighs. They got a spinning tool at about the same time that they got the fibers to spin. The Indian spindle was a slender, tapering stick made of juniper, mountain mahogany, or some other hard, straight-grained wood. The spindle was as long as the distance from the tip of the thumb to the tip of the middle finger of an outstretched hand. After the Spanish invasion, when Indians from Old Mexico came into the Southwest as Spanish slaves, there was a disk-shaped stone or clay weight attached to the base of the spindle, to weigh it down and make it revolve more evenly.

The spinner sat on the ground, in the same position he took for thigh spinning, with the spindle resting against his left

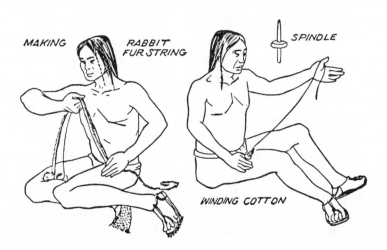

MAKING   RABBIT FUR STRING   SPINDLE

WINDING COTTON

knee. He held a tuft of fiber shaped like a little pillow between the thumb and forefinger of his right hand and laid it against the upper tip of the spindle. Then he twisted the spindle sharply forward with his left palm, at the same time pulling the thread away from the spindle and twisting it in the opposite direction from that in which the spindle turned. The thread was spun with a reverse, or double twist, that tightened and strengthened it. Some buffalo hair and dog hair was also spun with a spindle.

Naturally, with all their different kinds of string and thread, the Anasazi could make not only nets but fabrics. The Indians probably began with very simple textiles, but before long they began to make all kinds of cloth, some of it with extremely complicated plaiting or weaving patterns.

The first Anasazi cloth was not woven but was plaited like some of the Indian baskets. You sometimes hear plaited cloth called "finger woven," and much of it really is so fine and close that it looks as if a loom must have been used to make it.

If you examine the plaited fabrics closely, though, it is easy to see that they have no fixed warps. An element is a warp for a while, and then turns around and becomes a weft. The same thing happens in three-strand braiding. One string crosses the other two, over and under, like any weft. Then each of the other strings, in turn, crosses the first one, which has become a warp. Then the first strand becomes a weft again and recrosses the other two, which have become temporary warps.

Plaiting can be done with as many elements as the weaver wants to use. He can start with three, or he can start with a hundred, or he can start with any number in between. His braid can be a fraction of an inch wide, or it may be several feet across. It is a matter of knowing how, and of having time and patience enough to go on working.

Like baskets, cloth can be made with two or more twined weft elements. *Twined cloth*, as it is sometimes called for short, is a kind of halfway process between plaiting and true weaving. A twined fabric has a set of warps and a set of wefts, and the two sets are separate and distinct. However, twined cloth cannot be made on a loom. Sometimes a frame is used, but one is not necessary. The warps can be held in the hands of the worker, and the wefts passed over, under, and around them in the same movements as those made by the twining elements in basketry.

Loom weaving, and the making of true cloth, came rather late in Anasazi history. Like so many other important things the Anasazi knew about, it was invented or introduced about A.D. 750, at the time when the Indian cities were reaching their greatest development. True cloth is woven with a set of fixed warps, fastened to beams and moved with heddles. In finger weaving and twining, each weft must be passed over and under each warp separately. In true weaving, one set of warps is pulled forward, or upward, by pulling on the heddle through which the threads have been strung. The weft passes behind, or under, the whole set of warps at one time. The other heddle and its attached warps are drawn toward the weaver, and the weft is passed back behind, or under, that set. A weaver may

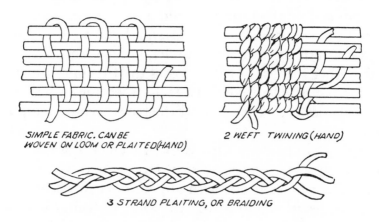

SIMPLE FABRIC. CAN BE
WOVEN ON LOOM OR PLAITED(HAND)

2 WEFT TWINING (HAND)

3 STRAND PLAITING, OR BRAIDING

work with two heddles and crossed warps, or he may use more. Most Indian cloth seems to have been woven with two heddles, but some patterns required as many as eight.

One of the great differences between the Old World and the New World—like the difference between wheat and corn, or between two- and three-strand cords—is in loom-making. Old World looms are horizontal. The warps are stretched flat before the worker, and the heddles move up and down. New World looms are vertical. The warps are stretched up and down, and the heddles can be pulled back and forth.

In Old World looms, the heddles are moved by foot treadles, and the wefts are wound on shuttles that slide across the loom face on a wooden bar. On New World looms, the heddles must be pulled forward by hand, and the wefts passed between the warps on a stick shuttle held by the weaver. Old World weaving is faster than that of the New World, but all true weaving is so much faster than plaiting or twining that the Anasazi must have been delighted with even the simplest looms.

Although weaving is the fastest textile process, plaiting and twining can produce more varied fabric designs. Each method has its own advantages. For that reason, the Anasazi used all of them, and the modern Indians still make plaited belts and twined rabbit-fur blankets. Here is an Indian weaving song:

SONG OF THE SKY LOOM

O our Mother the Earth, O our Father the Sky,
Your children are we, and with tired backs
We bring you the gifts you love.
May the warp be the white light of morning,
May the weft be the red light of evening,
May the fringes be the falling rain,
May the border be the standing rainbow.
Thus weave for us a garment of brightness,
That we may walk fittingly where birds sing.
That we may walk fittingly where grass is green.
O our Mother the Earth, O our Father the Sky.

Present-day Hopi Weaver

When the Anasazi men made cloth by the twining method, they did not need to use looms. They could lay the fibers on their knees, or on the ground in front of them, and work with the ends of the cords free. After a time, the men probably realized that they could work faster and the cloth they made would be smoother if the ends of the strings were fastened down. So they drove two rows of pegs into the ground, and ran the warps back and forth around each upright before they started work with the wefts.

Another way of making a frame, which the Anasazi probably used, is putting four pegs in the ground at the corners of a square. Then you can tie a cord between each pair of pegs and fasten the warps to the cord. If you put the warps *around* the cords, without tying the end of each strand but in a long, endless chain arrangement, you can move the cloth as it is made from one end of the frame to the other.

Usually, when people are making cloth with a frame, they have bobbins of wood or bone to use in passing the wefts over and under the warps. Some bobbins, a few with eyes, like needles, have been found in Anasazi ruins. Working with a bobbin is much faster and easier than trying to pass the wefts over and under the warps with your fingers.

We do not know when the great change came and the frame was lifted from its position parallel with the ground and set upright. We do know that the step must have taken place, for the Anasazi looms were made by fastening a heavy beam in the walls of a cave or kiva, across a corner, or by fastening one end of the beam in the wall and suspending the other from the ceiling. A second warp beam was supported by ropes tied to the first one or to the ceiling and hung just clear of the floor.

The warps passed around the two beams, which were actually strong poles. The warps were looped around as the warps on the frames were, so that they and the weaving could be shifted from time to time. The weaver sat on the floor or the ground before his loom with his heddles at about shoulder level. To start working, he twisted the end of the weft thread

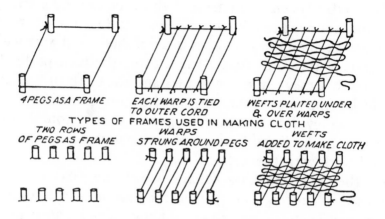

4 PEGS AS A FRAME EACH WARP IS TIED WEFTS PLAITED UNDER
       TO OUTER CORD   & OVER WARPS

TYPES OF FRAMES USED IN MAKING CLOTH

TWO ROWS   WARPS   WEFTS
OF PEGS AS FRAME STRUNG AROUND PEGS ADDED TO MAKE CLOTH

two or three times around the outside warp on the left-hand side. He pulled the first heddle toward him and passed the weft behind the set of warps that were moved forward by the heddle. Then, with a narrow, smoothly polished piece of juniper—it looked a little like a wooden sword—he pressed the weft down until it was firm and level in place, all across the face of the loom. He withdrew the wooden batten, as the piece of wood is called, and pulled the next heddle forward. He passed the weft back from right to left and then pressed the web firm with the batten.

The turns made by the weft threads around the outside warps are called the selvage of a piece of cloth, and it is important that each weft stretch evenly from selvage to selvage if the cloth is not to pull out of shape. So sometimes the Anasazi weavers used small wooden combs, as well as battens, to push the threads into place in the fabric. As the weaving moved up the face of the loom, it would gradually become too high off the ground for the weaver to reach comfortably. Then he could loosen the ropes that held the beams in place, and roll the cloth around the lower pole and stitch it around the lower pole. Each time the weaver shifted his web, he had to shift the heddles, too.

Cloth can be made with warps of one color and wefts of another. The warps can be of two colors, perhaps black and

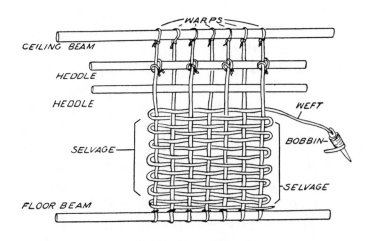

white, strung alternately. If the wefts are also of two or more colors, all kinds of checks and plaids can be made on a two-heddle loom. If more than two heddles are used, the weaving patterns can be even more complicated. Twills, like our satin, can be woven, and so can herringbone twills, like those in men's suits, or diamond twills, like the woven patterns in some coats and rugs. The Anasazi knew about and used all these different kinds of woven designs.

Spinning and weaving are pleasant work, and they can be done by several people working together in the same room. The men often took their spinning and weaving into the kivas, and in some of the old cities kivas have been found where two or three looms must have hung at the same time. Holes had been drilled in the ceilings, and ropes to hold the beam poles had been mortared into them with adobe mud. In some cases the mortar and ropes were still solidly in place almost a thousand years later.

One disadvantage of plaited or twined fabrics is that they cannot be cut. Each piece of textile must be made the exact size of the finished garment. The Anasazi apparently got so in the habit of producing fabrics in this way that they continued to work to size after they began to weave. The shape of a piece of cloth, as well as its size, was decided by the shape of the garment that was to be made from it.

The first Indian settlers in the Four Corners seem to have worn almost no clothing. Perhaps they wrapped up in hides when the weather was cold, although we are not sure that they did even that. The women wore little aprons, made with a plaited front piece and finished with a twisted string fringe that hung down to the knees front and back. The apron was tied around the waist of the wearer with a piece of string instead of a belt. The men and children, as far as we know, wore nothing at all, unless they had small breechclouts.

But everybody had the most beautiful sandals that could be made. These sandals were plaited, with very complicated designs on the upper sides of the soles. Of course the wearer's feet covered the designs and hid them, but everybody knew the patterns were there. On the undersides of the soles, next to the ground, other elaborate patterns were worked out in knots. The knots themselves were probably intended to thicken the sandal soles, protect the feet against stones and thorns, and give extra traction when people walked on slippery surfaces, such as sloping rocks or mud along the streams. There was no reason to make the sandal soles beautiful, for plain rows of knots would have worked just as well as the fancy designs, but the Anasazi loved beautiful things enough to make them even when they would not show. The Indians also fringed the toes of their sandals and tied their footgear in place with beautifully plaited cords. One cord made a loop across the toe of a sandal, and the foot was slipped under it. Another loop went across the sandal's heel, with the foot set in front of it. Then a third string was tied to the front one, passed around the outside of the ankle and under the heel strap, and fastened between the big and second toes to the front string. This held the sandal in place.

Long after they began to make and wear sandals, the Anasazi started producing plaited bags. They used yucca, sotol, or apocynum fibers, and sometimes combined the plant threads with animal yarns. These bags were worked with intricate geometric designs, in what is sometimes called "tapestry

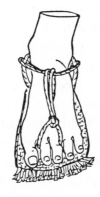

Three Types of Anasazi Sandals

work.'' It is a very fancy kind of plaiting and does resemble woven tapestry in appearance. The Indians must have prized the bags highly, for the owners saved their bags and mended them when they wore out. The Anasazi also had undecorated bags made of coarser fibers for everyday use. The heavy bags held corn and seeds; the fine ones may have been intended to hold jewelry or sacred articles.

At about the same time that they began making fine bags, the Anasazi also began to plait belts. At this time the women began to wear wider aprons, decorated with plaited designs, and they probably made the belts to hold up the aprons. Maybe the men and boys fastened breechclouts to their belts, and they almost certainly hung their knives from them. Plaited straps, like longer belts, were used as tumplines.

Rabbit-fur blankets became fashionable a little later. Most of the blankets were twined, with plain yucca warps that were hidden by the fluffy fur and yucca wefts. These blankets were much heavier than they looked and were as precious as the fine bags. Some Anasazi were wrapped in three or four fur blankets when they were buried, and their fine bags were laid in the graves with their owners. Such men must have been excellent hunters and good workers. Perhaps they were gardeners who raised extra corn to trade to their friends and relatives for fine textiles.

The fur blankets were all right in the winter but too warm for summer garments. Soon afterward the Anasazi began to weave on looms, and they produced blankets of yucca and other wild plant fibers, as well as of cotton. A few pieces of woven milkweed-fiber cloth have been found; and probably the priests or other important men had milkweed blankets, but we do not know about that. The blankets made from more ordinary fibers were precious enough, especially the cotton ones. Sometimes they were made for babies and sometimes for the important men. Perhaps the brides also wore them, as Hopi brides still do.

We think that the men may have become weavers because they had provided skins for their families to wear when they went hunting. Since the earliest garments were made of skins, it would seem like a natural thing for the men also to provide the clothing that became fashionable later. We know, too, that the men had plenty of time to spin and weave during the days of fall and winter, when the work in the fields was finished for the year. The women's work, cooking and cleaning, grinding cornmeal, caring for the babies, and making baskets and pottery, went on all through the year. The men's work in the gardens could only be done in the warm weather.

Besides the designs that were woven into the cloth, Anasazi blankets were decorated with painted designs, and at least one, found in one of the cave cities on Mesa Verde, is covered with a brown-and-white tie-and-dye design. It would be very interesting to know how often this method was used in the old, lost days, and whether more than one weaver ever experimented with it.

Some Anasazi men decorated their clothing and their wives' dresses with embroidered designs. At a later date, when Spanish women moved into the Southwest, the Indian women as well as the men learned to knit and crochet. Among other things that were made were long, footless stockings—really leggings—for the men to wear in the dances. Women and children took up the custom afterward. In some modern pueblos, the older people still wear such stockings with their moccasins, and the women make crocheted shirts for the men and boys to wear in dances.

In the early Spanish description of the Indians of the towns, we read that most of the people wore white cotton blankets unless they were doing especially hard or dirty work. A woman's dress was a single blanket, worn wrapped around her. The edges joined in an open seam on the right side, and the upper corners were tied or pinned on the right shoulder. The left shoulder was bare. Then a plaited or woven belt was pulled tight around the waist and tied in back, to hold the seam securely. Long afterward, when the Indians got silver and began to make pins from it, the women wore silver brooches to fasten

Woven Rug

the seams of their dresses from the armpit down to the knee, but they often relied on their broad belts to hold the seams in place on the right sides.

With their blankets, the women may have worn sandals at the time of the conquest. Later, they wore moccasins, made like those of some of the Indians of the Southern Plains, with hard rawhide soles and soft buckskin uppers. Still later, the women attached a whole deer hide to each moccasin and wound the skins tightly around their legs. In some of the pueblos the skins were left whole; in others they were cut into broad bandages, and the strips were wound around and around the wearers' legs. In either case, the bulkier, tighter, and smoother the wrappings were wound, the more fashionable the woman was. The soles of the moccasins were dyed black and were turned up all around the edges. If a woman wanted to look her best at a big dance or on some other important occasion, she spent a whole morning rubbing the tops of her leggings with white clay and painting around the soles with charcoal. For everyday, some Pueblo Indian women still wear moccasins with high tops of red-dyed buckskin and with black soles. These moccasins are fastened on with silver buttons—a solid row of them up the outside of each leg.

Some Indian women nowadays dress like everybody else, in dresses that they buy at stores. Many of the older Pueblo women prefer to make their dresses at home. They usually wear a long, straight underdress, with long sleeves. Ordinarily the blouses are made of cotton prints, with large, brightly colored patterns, but some women prefer plain colors. The sleeves are loose and open, with a ruffle or a band of lace around the wrist. Over this the women wear dresses, made of plain-colored cotton or of printed material with a different background, fastened over the right shoulder and under the left, like the old-time blanket dresses. The overdress is held in place with an old-fashioned belt. At ceremonials and festivals the women fasten large square pieces of silk prints or big bandanna handkerchiefs to their shoulders, and let them flutter down in back. And at celebrations they also wear cotton or silk

TEEN-AGE MARRIAGEABLE AGE MATRON GRANDMA
HOPI WOMEN'S HAIR-DOS

OTHER PUEBLO WOMEN'S STYLES: SIDE PART OR BANGS

MOST GIRLS UNDER TWELVE AROUND 500 A.D. ABOUT 1200

aprons, trimmed with lace and braid, tied around their waists.

In the early days, as we know, the Anasazi women cut their hair off for their husbands to use in rope-making. Later, the women must have told the men to use something else, for they began to let their hair grow long and to dress it very elaborately. The women washed their hair with yucca suds, rubbed it with deer's or bear's grease, and combed and brushed it with porcupine tails, bundles of sunflower seed heads, and bunches of stiff grass. In some Anasazi groups it was possible to tell whether or not a woman was married by the way she wore her hair. Unmarried women had theirs put up over willow hoops, one on either side of the face, in great whorls that were called squash blossoms. Married women wore their hair as most Indian women do today: parted in the middle, with Dutch bangs across their foreheads, a short lock against each cheek, and a club, tied with a strip of handwoven cloth at the nape of the neck.

The Spanish chronicles tell us that early Pueblo men wrapped their blankets around their shoulders and tied the upper corners together in front. The men wore belts and tied breechclouts to them, and they probably had moccasins to wear in wet, cold weather.

Children in the early days were dressed in little blankets or aprons, depending on whether they were boys or girls. They had their own small blankets to wear when the weather got chilly or they wanted to dress up. They had high-topped moccasins, as the grown people did.

After the Indians learned to raise sheep and to spin and weave from wool, they made woolen blankets to replace the cotton ones. They also learned to dye cloth with indigo, a plant dye the Spaniards used, and were very fond of its dark blue color. The Spaniards traded cloth dyed red with dried cochineal insects to the Indians, but this material was so rare and expensive it was only used for decoration. Cochineal-dyed yarn was often embroidered into the borders of the women's dark blue blanket dresses. The dresses, which were very beautiful, were also very precious, and were handed down from mother to daughter. Some Indian women still have heirloom dresses of this type.

For at least two hundred years after the Spanish conquest, most Pueblo men wore belts and breechclouts, blankets and moccasins, and their jewelry, but nothing else. Then some men began to wear shirts that hung almost to their knees, with the belts holding the shirts in place. Later, they made themselves cloth trousers—just two long tubes for the legs. They tied the tops of their pants to their belts and covered them with their breechclouts.

Nowadays Indian men usually wear Levi's and cotton shirts like other men in the Southwest. Sometimes they wear high boot-topped moccasins or cowboy boots; sometimes they wear shoes. Often the modern Indian men wear hats. Probably their Anasazi ancestors would laugh at them, going around with

ANASAZI MEN'S HAIR STYLES
BEARDS AND MUSTACHES APPARENTLY WERE PLUCKED

PUEBLO MEN'S HAIR STYLES

their hair covered.

The Anasazi ancestors were very proud of their hair, and the men certainly never cut theirs, no matter how badly they needed string! Instead, they washed it and brushed it and oiled it till it shone. They wore it, as their ancestors did, tied tightly at the napes of their necks. Sometimes a man braided a lock of hair on top of his head and let it hang to the side or over one eye. Some men parted their hair from front to back, in the center, then made a club over either ear. And some Anasazi men wore their hair in two braids, one over each shoulder.

The modern men of the pueblos usually wear their hair long, banged in front like the women's, and tied and bound at the napes of their necks. At Taos Pueblo the men often wear two braids, wrapped around and around with yarn or ribbon. In many pueblos a man with short hair cannot take part in certain ceremonies, and a boy who has had to cut his hair while he was away at school or in the army is required to let it grow again as soon as he comes home.

Even in the days when they wore sandals, and very few clothes, and the women hacked off their hair, the Anasazi made and wore jewelry. At first the Indians had only necklaces. They drilled holes in five or six shells and strung them on a twisted or braided cord. The men tied the strings around their necks like chokers. Later the Indians made pendants of single large shells, each with one or two holes drilled through the hinge end for the suspension cord.

The Anasazi took great pains to drill the shells without splitting or breaking them. The shells came from the Pacific Ocean, and they had been carried a long way, traded from one group of Indians to another, before they reached the Four Corners. Consequently, the shells were very rare, and the Indians regarded them as great treasures. Probably the Anasazi thought that shells which had come out of the great waters to the west were sacred and had magical powers. They might bring rain to the fields of the men who wore them.

In order to drill holes in the shells, the Anasazi men made very fine, sharp-pointed stone tools. At the upper end of a drill there was often a flange that could be fitted into a socket at the base of a wooden handle. The worker looped a string around the handle and tied the ends of the string to a short wooden bow. He laid the shell on a slab of stone and set the drill point in place against the shell. Then he rested his chin on the upper end of the drill handle, and pulled the bow back and forth with his hands. As the string moved, it caused the point of the drill to revolve against the shell and gradually pierce into it. If the worker wanted to hurry, he dipped the drill first in water and then in fine sand, to make it cut faster.

When the hole was drilled halfway through the shell, the worker turned his shell over and began drilling from the other side so the two holes would meet in the middle. In that way, the openings were equally large, and the shell was easier to string. Working from either side also reduced the risk of shattering the shell. Whenever an archeologist finds a shell or shell bead in the ruin of an Anasazi town, he holds it up to the light to see if the suspension-hole is hourglass shaped. In late years, the white traders brought in shell beads that had been pierced with power drills. In those beads, the holes go straight through from one side to another because they were made in a single process.

Shell bracelets were introduced to the Anasazi country from the south at about the same time that cotton appeared. A bracelet was made by drilling a series of holes around a large shell, about a quarter of an inch in from the edge. Then the solid center of the shell was knocked out, and the inner margin of the bracelet was ground smooth with wet sand. These bracelets were slipped over the hands and up the arms of their wearers. The piece of shell that had been broken out to make the bracelet was probably saved for bead-making.

The beads were made by breaking up the larger pieces of shell into fragments. Each little, angular scrap was separately drilled. Then the rough beads were tightly threaded on a sinew string. The worker laid the string of beads on a flat slab of sandstone and wet the surface thoroughly. He rolled the beads back and forth, between the palm of his hand and the stone, until he had ground off all the corners and the edges of the beads were smooth and round. Some shell beads were quite large, almost an inch across, while others were no bigger than pinheads. When the beads were strung in necklaces, they were graduated in size, from tiny ones at the ends to large

disks in the middle.

The Anasazi learned to work soft, solid stones in the same way that they worked shells, and to make pendants and beads of turquoise and jet. By the time the Indians began to build cities, they had necklaces and pendants, bracelets and earrings. A few men even had shell finger rings. The priests and other important men had pendants made of large shells with turquoise and jet inlay. The pieces of stone were carefully cut and polished, and were set into the grooves of the shells in beautiful designs. At Pueblo Bonito, in Chaco Canyon, one of the greatest of the ancient Indian cities, the jeweler also made pendants of cedar wood, inlaid with turquoise, jet, and red and white shell.

Turquoise and jet are found in many places in the Southwest. Very beautiful turquoise comes from the mines at Cerrillos (say-REE-yose), near Santa Fe, New Mexico. The best jet comes from beds near the Hopi towns. The Indians have known of the deposits for centuries. Far back in the veins of the Cerrillos deposits, far underground, stone hammers and knives that were dropped by Anasazi miners have been found. Today most Indians buy their turquoise at the trading posts that are located near the Indian towns.

Shell, turquoise, and jet were used in precious jewelry. The Anasazi also made less valuable ornaments, about like our costume jewelry. They made necklaces and bracelets of juniper berries and other seeds, and some men had pendants of deer hoofs. There were basketry flowers and disks to be worn as hair ornaments in ceremonies. The Anasazi also made ornaments of bright-colored feathers for the men to wear in their hair or on their arms or shoulders when they danced. They made tall wooden headdresses for the women to wear in ceremonial dances, carved and painted with blue and yellow and black and white earth colors, and decorated with tufts of white down feathers.

Unlike Indians in other parts of North America, the Anasazi did not wear a great deal of face paint. They and their descendants painted their faces and upper bodies for ceremonies but not for everyday. Color was always very important in the religion of the Indians of the Four Corners, and perhaps for that reason they wore it only on special, sacred occasions. And, unlike some other Indians, the Anasazi did not practice tattooing. Both men and women pierced their ears, and their children's ears, so they could wear earrings, and the custom is still being carried on today.

No matter how elaborate Anasazi weaving became, or how much beautiful jewelry the Indians wore, their clothing remained simple. Even after the women's dresses and the men's trousers were made from material purchased in the trading posts, the shapes of the garments were the same shapes that Anasazi garments had always been: they were straight pieces of material, folded on one side and sewed, or pinned, together on the other.

There was no reason why the Anasazi should change the cut of their clothes. The straight simple garments were easy to make and easy to wear, no material was wasted in cutting the clothing, and everybody dressed alike. All through their history, the Anasazi have believed that people are happiest if all members of a group have what they need and all work together equally for the good of everyone. It was as natural for the Indians to express their idea in their clothing as in their houses, the planning of their fields, and the way in which they saved their surplus crops in the community storehouse.

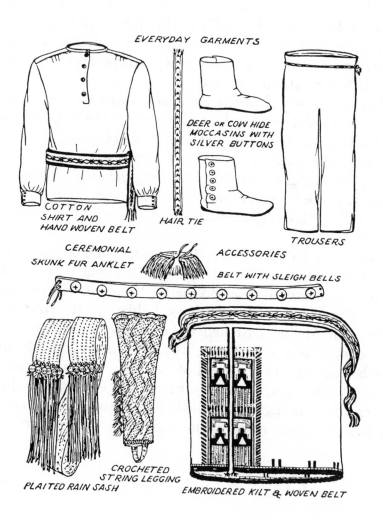

EVERYDAY GARMENTS

DEER OR COW HIDE
MOCCASINS WITH
SILVER BUTTONS

COTTON
SHIRT AND
HAND WOVEN BELT

HAIR TIE

TROUSERS

CEREMONIAL
SKUNK FUR ANKLET

ACCESSORIES

BELT WITH SLEIGH BELLS

CROCHETED
STRING LEGGING

PLAITED RAIN SASH

EMBROIDERED KILT & WOVEN BELT

Men's Wear

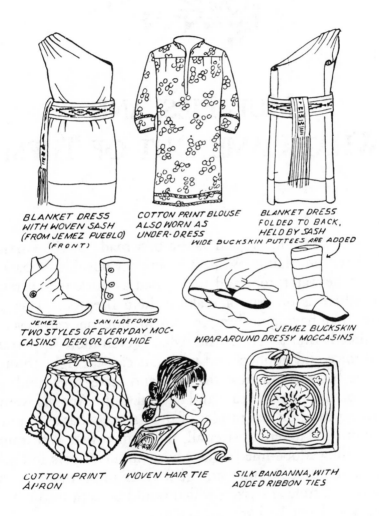

BLANKET DRESS
WITH WOVEN SASH
(FROM JEMEZ PUEBLO)
(FRONT)

COTTON PRINT BLOUSE
ALSO WORN AS
UNDER-DRESS

BLANKET DRESS
FOLDED TO BACK,
HELD BY SASH

WIDE BUCKSKIN PUTTEES ARE ADDED

JEMEZ   SAN ILDEFONSO
TWO STYLES OF EVERYDAY MOC-
CASINS DEER OR COW HIDE

JEMEZ BUCKSKIN
WRAP AROUND DRESSY MOCCASINS

COTTON PRINT
APRON

WOVEN HAIR TIE

SILK BANDANNA, WITH
ADDED RIBBON TIES

Women's Wear

MUD PIES, AND
WHAT CAME OUT OF THEM

EVEN BASKETS as good as the best made by the Anasazi have some faults. While it is perfectly possible for baskets to be waterproof and to be used as buckets and reservoirs, there is no way of making them fireproof. They are better than having nothing to cook in, but they can never be set directly over a flame. And, what is even more important, field mice and gophers and pack rats can eat right through storage baskets and steal the corn and seeds they hold.

Probably it seemed easy and natural to the Anasazi women to smear mud on the insides of their storage baskets, and so keep out the rodents. After all, the women were accustomed to building adobe-lined storage boxes in their floors and walls. There would be nothing strange to them in putting an adobe lining in a storage basket, which would be kept in the house and would not be likely to get wet.

As a matter of fact, the women were pleased with the idea of clay containers, and they must have experimented with them a lot. They saw that plain mud would stick to the sides of the basket as long as it was wet, but that as soon as it began to dry the adobe would crack and chip and start to peel away from the basketry walls. So some woman tried mixing a little grass and a few pebbles in her adobe, and she soon found out that by distributing the moisture and slowly drying in this way she got a more durable inner wall. As time went on, and more women experimented with the process, they learned that sand was the best substance to mix with the clay.

Even with this improvement, the Anasazi lacked real pottery. They learned to lift the dried mud shells out of the baskets in which they had been formed, and to use the earthenware bowls in housekeeping. But the women also learned that if the bowls got wet, or even slightly damp, they would melt. Any seeds the bowl held would be left lying on the floor in a mud puddle.

How the women learned to bake their bowls is still a mystery. Archeologists once thought that perhaps there was a house fire which destroyed everything the family owned except the mud linings in some of the baskets. When the flames died down and the ashes of the roof and wall supports cooled off, the first pottery bowls were found in the ruins and were discovered to be waterproof.

The trouble with this theory is that there would have had to be so many fires. One set of baked basket-linings would never have been enough to convince anybody that pottery had been discovered. And the Anasazi were sensible, busy people. They wouldn't have been likely to burn a house down every time they needed a new set of mouse-proof storage jars. Houses were too hard to build, and it took too long to put a house up, for anyone to want to burn it down again.

Another explanation is that pottery, like weaving and cotton and corn, came to the Anasazi from Indians living to the south of them. But the difficulty with this idea is that the first Indian pottery was too thick and heavy to have been carried around easily. Perhaps the *idea* traveled from southern Arizona to the Four Corners, about A.D. 300, the time Mohammed lived, and the pottery itself did not.

At any rate, in the layers of earth and artifacts in the Anasazi caves and cave houses, archeologists have found every stage in the development of pottery in sequence. First the baskets; then the thick, unfired, mud storage jars; then crude, fire-baked bowls and jars; and then finer and thinner and more beautifully decorated wares.

Long before archeologists knew about tree-ring dating, they used pottery to date the main events of Anasazi life. They found that the first pottery appeared about the time that the Indians began living in pit house villages, in about A.D. 300. From then on, each time that there was a real change in the way the Anasazi lived, there was also a change in the manner in which their pottery was made or decorated.

Not only that. The archeologists discovered that each group of Indians made their own special kind of pottery. That is just as true today as it was eleven hundred years ago, when Charlemagne ruled France. The Indians who live in San Ildefonso Pueblo now make pottery that is entirely different from that made by the women of Acoma or Zia or the Hopi villages. And none of the others make pottery that is identical with that of any other pueblo.

By looking at a piece of southwestern Indian pottery, an expert can tell right away when and where it was made, and can generally say what the vessel was to be used for. If it is a piece made by one of the famous modern potters—Nampeyo, the Hopi, or Trínita of Zia, or Severa of Santa Clara, or María of San Ildefonso—the workmanship is unmistakable even when the potter has neglected to sign her name on the bottom of the piece. A few of the ancient Anasazi potters were so skillful that even though archeologists do not know the workers' names, they can still recognize a particular woman's work whenever an example of it is discovered.

Right from the start, Anasazi potters have made their pottery by the same method. The women of today are sure that what was good enough for all their great-grandmothers is good enough for them.

The first step in making pottery is getting the right clay. The Anasazi were lucky in this because they lived in an area where there was plenty of clay suitable for pottery-making. They also had beds of fine sand to mix with the clay, within easy reach. The women could go out and get a supply of material whenever they needed it.

Probably the women watched the banks of the streams, when they went for water, and noticed where the clay held hard and firm the imprint of a foot or the bottom of a water basket. In the same way, the Anasazi women found where the best clay was located, and could go to it easily whenever they needed mud to plaster a house, or seal a storage pit, or line a basket, or, later, make a jar.

Before the clay could be used, the potter's first job was to make sure her material was thoroughly clean. First, she worked water into the clay to wash it. The little sticks and bits of grass and weeds that were mixed up in the mud rose to the top of her bowl or basket and floated there. It was easy to skim the rubbish off with a twist of grass or a small basketry scoop. Pebbles and hard, insoluble lumps of clay sank to the bottom of the container. The liquid mud could be poured away from them into another vessel. When the clay was washed clean, the worker poured it into a large vessel to let the water evaporate. It seems likely that she used a basket for this purpose. That would be faster and better than a pottery jar.

When the clay had dried out into a good hard lump, the potter was ready for the next step. She broke her large lump into smaller pieces, using a stone hammer. Then the Indian woman ground the fragments of clay to powder on her kitchen metates. Modern Indian potters still use metates for clay-grinding because they say that cornmeal ground on the same metate is better. The surface of the stone becomes smoother and more even after clay has been worked on it.

A fine sand *temper*, as it is called, was mixed with the powdered clay while they were both still dry. It is hard to give a rule about adding sand, for most Indian women say they put in "enough to make the clay right." A very small proportion of the sand would be enough to spread the fine particles of clay apart and to reinforce the mixture.

Sand is not the only tempering material the Indians of the Southwest have used. As we know already, the first tempers were grass and pebbles. For a long time the women ground

ACOMA

SANTO DOMINGO

WATER JAR   SANTA CLARA JAR   MEAL BOWL

up their broken pottery to use for temper. Sand was the easiest material to get in the Four Corners, and the women soon discovered that it was as effective as anything else, so it eventually replaced all other tempers.

When the mixture of sand and clay felt "right" between her fingers, the potter began to add water and to mix her material into a smooth, thick paste. This part of the work was very slow and particular. The woman added a few drops of water at a time, and mixed and stirred and felt and even tasted her compound to make sure all the air was worked out of it and it was exactly the way she wanted it to be. When the clay was precisely right, the woman covered it with a wet cloth or a piece of damp buckskin, and went away and left it alone for several days.

This "ripening" or "seasoning" of the clay was a very important process, although it must have been trying for a woman who had an idea about a bowl in her mind and wanted to work it out. But the Indian women always took their time. They knew it was better to work slowly and make a fine bowl than to rush through the job and end with a poor one. So they waited for the clay to ripen, and to blend thoroughly with the sand and water. They watched the wrapping around the clay and dampened the cover whenever it began to dry out.

When the clay was ready, the woman sat down on the floor by the container of damp clay. She dipped her hands in a bowl of water, and she was careful always to work with wet hands so the clay would not stick to her fingers and spoil the bowl.

The potter took a small piece of clay and kneaded it like a roll, to work out any tiny air bubbles that might be left in the mixture. Even one could swell when it got hot in the pottery fire, and break or distort the shape of the bowl.

Next the woman made a ball of clay, and slapped and turned the ball between her palms until she had made a round, flat pancake. She set this in the bottom of an old bowl or basket and shaped the clay to fit the curve of the mold that rested on the ground before her.

Then the potter took another piece of clay and again worked out the bubbles so the finished piece would not crack. She rolled this piece between her palms into a long, even sausage. She fitted the sausage to the edge of the pancake, moistening the seam with water, and then pressing it firmly to fasten the strip of clay in place. Then she made another sausage and fitted it on above the first. She was careful not to join the ends above the joint of the first coil. The woman continued to add coils to the walls of the bowl until it was almost as tall as it was meant to be. Sometimes the potter left the coils as they were and let them show on the sides of the finished bowl.

Then the woman began to smooth the walls of her vessel. She dampened a flat piece of wild gourd shell or stone or old pottery and worked around the bowl inside and out, holding the tool in her right hand and laying her left palm against the inner surface. The base in which her work was set turned on the ground before her as she worked, so she was able to make the clay walls even in thickness.

As the clay was smoothed and thinned, it seemed to stretch, and its shape could be changed a little. If the woman wanted a bowl, she smoothed off the top coil carefully, and her work was finished. If she wanted to make a water jar, she built the vessel upward with slightly thicker coils, to make the shoulder and rim. If she wanted a bottle, she added more coils and built a neck up from the rim of the jar. Perhaps while she worked she sang a song something like this:

THE SONG OF THE HUMMING POTTER

Big gray clouds cover the sky.
See. Little white clouds drift along the edge of the
world.
After a while the blue sky will come out again.
Before blue covers the world,
I should finish the bowl.
Perhaps I will not make a bowl.
A jar would be nice—a storage jar with a long neck.
But I think I will make a bowl
With painted water snakes around its rim.
Then my little boy can eat his mush
And look at the painted snakes.

Bowls and jars were shaped most often by southwestern potters, but the women also made bottles, dippers, and mugs. A few potters made fancy shapes: effigies of animals or plants or people. Sometimes a woman made a foot-shaped or moccasin-shaped vessel, but these were probably meant to be used in ceremonies. The vessels could be of any size, from delicate miniatures to enormous storage jars that would hold ten or fifteen gallons of seeds or water.

Whatever the size or shape of the vessel, it had to dry out thoroughly after it had been shaped. The women dried their pottery indoors in bad weather, but on good days they set the pieces outside to dry. The potters were careful not to put damp vessels in the sun or wind but to let the water evaporate slowly in a still, shady spot. Drying took several days, and after the pottery dried it was hard enough to keep for some time without firing, if it were kept dry. Often the women made and dried several pieces of pottery at a time and kept them to decorate later. It might be several months after the vessels were made that the worker fired her wares.

Decorating the pottery was the most interesting part of the work. We can be sure of this because the women invented several different ways of decorating, and because they spent enough time and thought on decoration to become great and famous artists. In the last thirty years, some men have painted pottery that their wives made. The custom may have originated long ago, but we have no record of it.

The earliest wares made in the Four Corners were plain, but before long the women began to paint designs on their pottery. They rubbed the outer surface of a vessel smooth, probably with fine sandstone or loose sand, and then began to paint. The first painted decorations were geometric designs. The vessels look as if the women wanted to copy the patterns of the baskets the pottery was going to replace. The Anasazi women made diamonds and triangles and herringbones and straight lines, but no curves. That was because they hadn't yet seen curved designs.

It would take too long to describe all the different styles of pottery decoration the Anasazi women thought up. At one time, they tried making jars and bottles with plain bodies and decorative coils on the necks. At another period, about the time when William the Conqueror landed in England, pottery with grooves around it was fashionable. The grooves were made by pressing a thumbnail into the damp clay of the vessel. Another style that developed a little later had geometric designs dented into the grooves while the clay was still wet. The patterns on this thumbnail-indented pottery, as it is called, look so much like the patterns on plaited baskets that the women seem to have copied them from the familiar containers. You would almost expect it to be older than the painted wares, instead of newer.

Later on, about the time when printing was invented in Europe, painting pottery became fashionable again, and it has continued to be the most important way of decorating pottery in the Indian towns of the Southwest. Often the women put a thin wash, or *slip,* of paint over an entire vessel, as a background for other painted designs. Sometimes the slip is

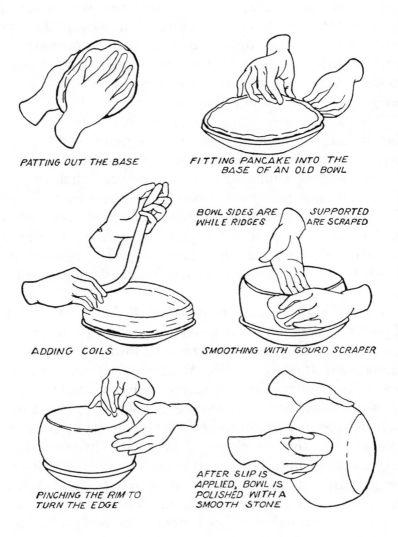

PATTING OUT THE BASE

FITTING PANCAKE INTO THE
BASE OF AN OLD BOWL

ADDING COILS

BOWL SIDES ARE   SUPPORTED
WHILE RIDGES   ARE SCRAPED

SMOOTHING WITH GOURD SCRAPER

PINCHING THE RIM TO
TURN THE EDGE

AFTER SLIP IS
APPLIED, BOWL IS
POLISHED WITH A
SMOOTH STONE

How to Make Pottery

rubbed with a smooth stone until it is almost as shiny but not as hard as a true glaze. Polished slipped vessels are very beautiful without any other decoration. Sometimes the potters do not apply slips but paint directly on the smoothed clay of their bowls or jars.

The Anasazi were very lucky, for there was earth of many different colors in their country. Red, blue, white, gray, and several yellows were easy to find. However, the women needed a good black, and they discovered that if they boiled the seedpods of guaco (WAH-ko), the Rocky Mountain bee plant, till it made a syrup and painted designs on the pottery with that, the vegetable color would burn (or carbonize) when the pottery was fired. Then the wares were decorated with a beautiful black.

For a long time the Indian women continued to use angular geometric designs on their pottery. This was making their work harder than it needed to be. The women made their paintbrushes out of fine, dry yucca-leaf ribs, chewed until they were soft and pliable at the lower end, while the upper end was left stiff, for a handle. This made a delicate brush, and the women could paint hairlines if they wanted to. Since they were applied to curved surfaces, it was natural for the brushes to follow the curves of the bowls or jars. It would have been equally natural, and much easier, for the women to paint curved designs. Apparently they didn't want to until fairly late in their history, for even today many of the designs on southwestern Indian pottery are angular, regardless of the curves of the vessels they decorate.

Firing the pottery was the last and most difficult stage in making it. Having the right kind of weather was most important for good firing. If the air was still, the smoke from the fire rose straight in the air, and the pottery colors were clear and unsmudged. On a windy day, when the smoke was blown back toward the fire, it could leave a smear of black smoke all over the vessels. About 1919, María and Júlian (HOO-lee-ahn) Martinez, of San Ildefonso, began making a new kind of black pottery. They smothered the fire with sheep or cow manure so that a dense black smoke would settle on their jars and bowls. But even after Mr. and Mrs. Martinez began to sell their all-black pottery to collectors they continued to make some red and painted wares by the old-fashioned, open-fire method.

When an Indian woman wanted to fire colored pottery, she first laid a bed of stones and sherds of broken pottery on the ground. The fire bed had two purposes: it distributed the heat so the pottery fired evenly; and it kept the wares from falling on the ground and breaking. Then the woman laid her fire with dry juniper and piñon wood and set the pottery carefully in place. She piled more wood over the vessels. Then she sprinkled the pottery and the firewood with cornmeal and prayed to the Powers Above to bless her work and make it good. At last she lit the fire. While the wood blazed, the potter watched the fire carefully, to make sure it burned evenly.

Wood fires burn brightly and quickly, but they do not get as hot as coal or gas fires. Most southwestern Indian pottery was fired at a temperature of about one thousand degrees. This was hot enough to harden the clay and make it durable but not hot enough to melt its surface particles and make a glazed finish. Just before the Spanish conquest, in about 1400, some of the Indians learned to make a mixture of sand, water, and other materials that would melt in the heat of the fires and would cause the vessels to glaze. Apparently the glaze was hard to mix or its materials were scarce, for no Indian vessel with an all-over glaze has yet been found. Instead, glaze designs were painted on the bowls and jars. They were rather carelessly done and look very much as if the potters were still experimenting with this method of decoration.

The Anasazi women seem to have enjoyed making pottery even more than they had basket-making. They turned out tons and tons of vessels. Thousands of specimens have been found whole in the ruins of the Anasazi cities, and the fragments of millions of pieces of pottery were dumped on the slopes in front of the caves or thrown in trash piles outside the walls of the cities that were built in the open.

Firing Pottery

The little girls worked along with their mothers, for we find their beginning work as well as the finished products of the grown women. The first tiny dishes a girl made were probably used as toys. Later, the girl might make a bowl to hold her mush, and perhaps after that she made another mush bowl for her baby brother or sister. By the time she was a young woman, and getting ready to keep house and raise a family of her own, she was able to make her own cooking utensils and tableware.

When the Indian men went on trading trips for shells or salt or buffalo hides and meat, they took pottery with them. Perhaps when a man left home he carried a supply of water in a pottery canteen or had some meal in a bowl with a piece of deerskin tied across its top. Then, when he reached his destination, the trader found someone who wanted one of his containers. He exchanged the bottle or bowl for whatever he wanted. Sometimes one of these men must have traded one piece of pottery for another, so he could take a new piece home to show his wife what other workers made. Archeologists find fragments of pottery in burials and dumps hundreds of miles from where they were originally made.

The modern Pueblo Indians carry on this same pottery trading. If a woman goes to visit a friend, she takes a piece of pottery with her for a hostess gift. When the visitor starts home, she will probably receive a piece of pottery to take with her. Or when a young couple marries, friends in Indian towns send them pottery for their new household. Even non-Indians help to spread Indian pottery, for they buy pieces of it to decorate their own homes or to give to their friends. Maybe thousands of years from now an archeologist excavating in New York will dig up a southwestern Indian bowl on Fifth Avenue. Perhaps the scientist of the future will know from our records when and where the bowl was made. Perhaps he will think that one twentieth-century artist knew how to make such things. Or he may say, as our archeologists must often say, that it is a trade piece and hope that at some future date he will learn where it was made.

AN ALL-AMERICAN COOKBOOK

HE ANASAZI gave as much thought and care to preparing their food as to everything else that they did. Indian women were proud of being good cooks and of serving good meals to their families.

From the time they settled in the Four Corners until the present, these Indians have had and used rather complicated kitchen equipment. In the very earliest days, when they may have expected to move on before the next winter, the women used whatever they could find. If there were a depression in a flat rock, like a bowl, a woman filled it with seeds. Then she pounded the seeds with another stone until she cracked their outer hulls. She tossed handfuls of crushed-seed meal in the air, so the hulls were blown away and the flour fell on a clean deerskin ready for use.

About the same time that they learned to grind seeds for meal, the Indian women discovered how to make fireless cookers. A woman dug a hole in the ground, making it about eighteen inches deep and about twelve inches across. She lined the pit with a deerskin, with the flesh side turned toward the middle. She put her meat or ground-up seeds or both in the skin with some water. Then she heated stones in the family campfire, and when they were red hot she lifted them on forked sticks and dropped them, one at a time, into the cooking pit.

This method of cooking was faster than it sounds. The only slow, difficult part of it was finding the right kind of stones, to be sure that they would not explode when they got hot. Probably the women saved their stones and carried them, wrapped in a bundle made of the cooking skin, tied in a net and slung from a tumpline. Perhaps the forked sticks to lift the stones were tied to the outside of the bundle.

Before very long, someone probably noticed that if the seeds were heated before they were pounded, the hulls split more easily and the seeds tasted better. Then the women began to make parching trays—wide, flat, flexible baskets—as part of their kitchen equipment. When the women wanted to cook, they spread seeds on the trays and then dropped live coals on the seeds. They twisted the baskets with their hands so that seeds and coals were tossed together and kept moving quickly around on the tray. A good cook could use a parching tray for a long time before it became so badly scorched that she had to throw it away.

This was at the time when basket-making was flourishing in the Four Corners. Fine, tight, waterproof baskets were used for stone-boiling, instead of deerskins. The family ate and drank out of basketry bowls and cups; they carried their water from the springs in pitch-covered baskets and stored it in special conical baskets set in holes in their floors. There were carrying baskets and gathering baskets and basket scoops, as well as the parching trays. The women also made flat baskets on which they tossed their pounded seeds up and down, so the broken hulls could be blown away. There were basketry ladles to dish up stew or mush, and basketry spoons with which to eat. The whole kitchen was supplied with basket utensils.

The biggest change in the kitchen equipment was in the grinding stones. The Anasazi lived in permanent houses now, and the women had places to keep things. They began to set the grinding stones up in the houses. They needed the stones every day now that they had corn to grind.

When she built a new house or refurnished her kitchen, a woman dug three square holes, like boxes, in its floor. She lined each hole with adobe, or with flat, smooth stones set in adobe. Then she put a flat stone slab in the box and mortared it in place, so it slanted upward from the front of the box to the back. It took a long time to work the surface of one stone smooth by rubbing it with another. The first stone was the coarsest and was usually used first to crack and break the corn. The surface of the second stone was smoother, and that of the third was almost slippery. As a stone became smoother from being used more often, it was moved over to another box. When the women died, their daughters inherited their grinding stones. When a young woman married, her mother might divide stones with her, so that each of them had a new, coarse, cracking stone and an older, smoother one for finishing. We call the flat grinding slabs metates (may-TAH-tays), which is an Aztec Indian word the Spaniards brought north from Mexico with them. The smaller stones with which the miller rubs the corn against the metates are called manos (MAH-nose), which is the Spanish word for hands. The set is called the *molino* (moe-LEE-noe), the Spanish name for a mill.

When she used her metates, a woman knelt on the floor

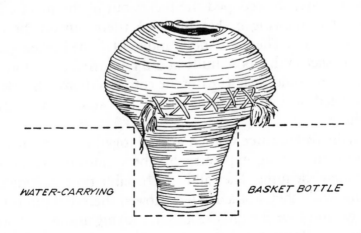

WATER-CARRYING   BASKET BOTTLE

behind the first stone, with her knees folded and her legs sticking straight out behind her. She held the mano in both hands
and brought it down on the corn she had spread on the stone.
She pushed the mano down and away from her, toward the
front of the box, bending forward from her waist. She swung
up and down, back and forth, grinding her corn, in time to
all kinds of little songs that she sang to make the work go faster.

CORN-GRINDING SONG

Lovely! See the cloud, the cloud appear!
Lovely! See the rain, the rain draw near!
Who spoke?
It was the little corn-ear
High on the tip of the stalk,
Saying, while it looked at me,
Talking, aloft there—
"Ah, perhaps the floods
Hither moving—
Ah, may the floods come this way!"

When the woman had broken the grains of corn on the
coarse metate, she scooped the pieces out of the metate box
onto her winnowing basket and took them out on the roof
or into the yard. There she shook and swirled the broken grains
in the basket so the loose hulls would be carried away and only the grain would be left. After the corn was thoroughly clean,
she carried it back downstairs for the second and third
grindings.

Usually two or three women worked together at the metates
and sent their daughters out with the winnowing baskets to
shake away the hulls. They all had a sociable time, talking and
singing while they worked. They showed their daughters how
to grind and gave the girls lessons in cooking as the work went
along. It was fortunate that the women were able to make their

work so pleasant, for each of them had many hours of grinding to do each day. Usually the women ground corn for old or sick people, as well as for their own families.

Even nowadays, when the Indians can shop in stores and buy commercially ground cornmeal whenever they want it, most older women keep their metates set up in their kitchens. They say that corn ground on a metate tastes better.

The Anasazi did not use much salt in their cooking, if we can judge by their modern descendants. Still, the Indians knew about salt and knew it was important, for it was like cornmeal and bean meal and dried meat—a food that was carried into the kivas for the ceremonial feasts. The men brought salt home when they went on trading trips to the tribes to the east or south of them. The Plains Indians, to the east, gathered salt from the salt-beds of Oklahoma, Kansas, and Texas, while the southern tribes brought theirs from the Pacific Ocean. There was a salt deposit in a canyon in the Hopi country, and the people of the western pueblos made long, difficult journeys to bring back rock salt to their villages. Even today, the best present you can bring a Pueblo Indian friend is a bag of coarse, lumpy rock salt, for only rock salt may be taken into the kivas. It is considered a "natural," or uncultivated, food.

Many of the dishes the Pueblo Indian women cook and serve today have been passed on from mother to daughter to great-great-granddaughter since Anasazi times. The one that is prepared most often is cornmeal mush, which the Indians call *atole* (ah-TOE-lay). This is made with one cup of coarsely ground yellow or white cornmeal, stirred into three cups of water, and cooked slowly till it is thick and smooth. Some cooks put salt in the water when it starts to boil; others add the salt when the *atole* is about half done. Like our cooks, the Indian women have no rule about the amount of salt. "Till it tastes right," they say.

Another very old dish that the Pueblo Indians still make and enjoy is hominy. The women use dried white corn to make it. They shell the ears of corn and stir the grains into a thin mixture of water and piñon wood ashes. That is strong lye,

Pueblo Kitchen

ANASAZI LADLE

and it must be handled carefully. When the corn has soaked in the lye solution for a few minutes, the hulls will pop off the kernels if the grains are squeezed between thumb and forefinger. When the corn reaches that point, the woman pours off the lye water and washes the grains thoroughly in fresh cold water to remove the hulls. Hominy can be cooked and eaten as soon as the water it is washed in is clear, or the grains can be dried and saved to be used later. Hominy grains can be cooked whole; or they can be broken and ground on the metates and the grits used to replace cornmeal in many recipes.

For great feasts, or when they were entertaining important guests, the Anasazi probably made the kind of corn bread that the Hopi call *piki* (PEE-kee). The woman of the house needed a special griddle for *piki*-making. The griddle was a thin, even, perfectly smooth slab of soapstone. Soapstone was always hard to find in the Southwest, and very few carvers have ever known how to work with it. As a result, *piki* griddles have always been rare and precious. Those who know how to make them can trade griddles for food or deerskins or bows and arrows whenever they want to.

When a woman wants to make *piki*, she prepares a very thin watery mixture of cornmeal and water. The cook can use red, blue, or white cornmeal for this. For an extra big party she makes a bowl of mush of each color. The woman sets the bowl on the right-hand side of the fireplace. She heats the *piki* stone as hot as she can get it—until if she drops a drop of water on the stone it rolls around like a ball. Then she dips her right hand in the bowl of mush and smears it over the surface of the hot stone. As the cook lifts her right hand, she rolls the edge of the smear of cornmeal with the fingers of the left hand. As the bread is baked through by the time she lifts her hand, she can peel the sheet of bread off the griddle, roll it up like a pancake, and then lay it on a basketry tray to cool. It takes a lot of practice to be able to make *piki* without burning your hands. Women who know how often trade their bread to their friends and neighbors for other articles they or their families need.

The Indians made tamales for special occasions, also. At first they made just plain tamales; then, after the Spaniards imported chile peppers and garlic and onions from Mexico into the Southwest, the Pueblo Indians began to make hot tamales. To make tamales, a woman made a thick mush with white cornmeal. She spread the mush out on clean, soft cornhusks—the ones that had grown next to the ears of the corn. Over the mush, the woman put a layer of beans, or ground meat, or dried fruit mixed with honey. Then she rolled the cornhusk and the mush together, around the filling, and tied the ends of the little package tightly. She could cook the tortillas either by boiling them in water or soup, or by baking them on a flat stone by the fire. She did not use the *piki* stone for tortillas. Nothing but *piki* could ever be baked on it.

The Indian women dried most of the food they gathered in the mountains or that the men raised for winter use. Wild seeds were dry before they could be gathered, and all that the women had to do with them was clean them and put them away. Wild berries or fruits were mashed with stone hammers, and then pressed into little flat cakes and spread out on the housetops in the sun to dry. Later, when the Spaniards showed the Indians how to raise garden and orchard fruits, the women cut up the apples, pears, peaches, and apricots and spread them out in the sun to dry. Every day the drying fruit was turned, usually with a wooden paddle, so that it would dry evenly. Then it was sacked up,

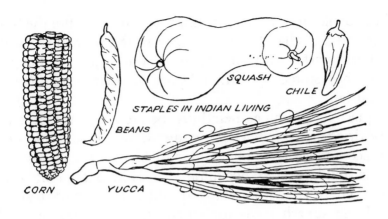

STAPLES IN INDIAN LIVING

SQUASH

CHILE

BEANS

CORN

YUCCA

and the bags were hung from the rafters of the storeroom; or sometimes the fruit was packed in lidded baskets for storage.

The Anasazi women gathered some corn for roasting ears and let the rest of the crop ripen on the stalks. They cleaned the husks and silk away from the ripe ears, braided the husks back from the stem, and made bunches or long strings of corn to keep. The corn hung outside the house till the time when the first snow was about to fall, and then was brought inside and hung from the rafters of the storeroom. Sometimes the women dried their corn by cutting it off the ears or shelling it off grain by grain. The cut corn was spread out in the sun like fruit, to dry thoroughly, before it was stored in bags or baskets for the winter.

Kidney beans, and speckled pinto beans, and hard little white navy beans, and the big, flat yellow narrow beans were pulled from the ground vines, roots and all. They were thrown down in heaps on clean ground, and the vines and husks were turned in the sun until they were dry. After that the people trampled on the vines, or, after they had farm animals, drove their cows and horses around and around over the crop to shake the beans out of the hulls. Then the women gathered up the stalks and hulls and burned them. The women saved the ashes to spread on the cornfields in the spring, for bean ashes contain valuable elements and make good fertilizer. After the bean vines and hulls had been cleared away, the women swept up the beans with special brooms made out of juniper boughs. Then they stored the dried beans in their storerooms in special jars.

Squash had to be gathered just before it ripened, if it was to be dried and saved. The ripe squash was too soft, and went to pieces too easily, to be handled much. But the almost-ripe squash could be sliced, or cut round and round into long strips, and then dried without any trouble. The Anasazi always saved the squash seeds for replanting, and they probably used them to flavor some of their corn dishes, as modern Indian women do.

The Indians dried meat as well as vegetables. They stripped the meat off the bones and sliced it as thin as tissue paper. Then they hung the slices on a wooden framework in the sun so the air could get to it from all sides. The meat turned black and hard, and it did not look very appetizing when it was sun-dried, but it was good food.

When the women wanted to cook dried meat, they first broke and pounded the large pieces on the coarse metates. Then they used the meat meal in hash, or to flavor tamales, and picked out the larger pieces that broke off to make stews. Sometimes the women made stews from fresh rabbit or squirrel or deer meat, and sometimes they roasted their meat by putting small pieces on sticks and toasting them over the coals, as we toast marshmallows.

The Anasazi knew about and used a long list of wild foods. They gathered cactus fruits and ate them fresh or dried. The women gathered the yucca seedpods at the same time that they got yucca leaves to make string and mats and baskets. A little later in the year, the women dug yucca roots to use for soap. They shook the dirt off and then pounded the roots thoroughly. When a piece of root was swished through a bowl of water three or four times, it made a fine, rich lather. Many Indian women today use yucca instead of commercial shampoos to wash their hair.

There were wild plums in the Anasazi country, and lots of chokecherries and a few wild grapes along the streams. In a few places in the mountain valleys there were wild strawberries and blackberries; and in many places black currants or bush gooseberries grew wild.

The Anasazi knew about Jerusalem artichokes, which are a root vegetable rather like potatoes, and they knew how to dig for wild turnips. They dried the wild vegetables for winter use, when they found a good supply.

In some places in the Four Corners there were oak trees that bore edible acorns. Not all acorns are good to eat, and some Indians must have had pretty bad stomachaches before they found a safe kind. The same thing was probably true of the mushrooms and fungi that occasionally grew in the woods and on the trunks of trees.

The best of all the nuts, and the easiest to get, were the piñon nuts—the kind that are sold in our stores under the name of pine nuts or Indian nuts. The nuts are tiny, and the weather has to be just right all year or the trees will not bear, so piñon nuts are always a treat when you can get them.

In a good piñon year the hillsides are covered with the little, low-growing pine trees, and each tree is covered with small, fat cones. As the nuts ripen, the cones pop open and scatter the nuts all over the ground until they lie thick on the mountainside. Then all the Indians go out to gather piñon nuts, and so do the squirrels and chipmunks and bears. Often people find the hole where a ground squirrel or chipmunk has stored his piñon nuts and are able to pick up a bushel at a time.

Piñon nuts are good just as they come from the tree, or roasted, or as flavoring in vegetable and meat dishes. The nuts are high in oil, and in cold winters like those in the Four Corners it is important for everybody to eat some fat every day. The Indian way of eating piñon nuts is to put them, hulls and all, in your mouth on one side, crack them with your teeth, swallow the nut meats, and spit the hulls out on the other side. When you can leave a solid line of piñon hulls behind you to show where you walked, you are a good Indian nut-cracker.

The Anasazi were intelligent people, for they raised gardens that gave them a well-balanced diet. The beans were a good source of protein, the food substance that makes good blood and strong bones. That was a good thing, since the Indians had a rather scanty supply of meat. Corn gave them starch, which is one of the carbohydrates. And they got plenty of vitamins from both these vegetables and from the squash and wild fruits and vegetables they ate.

The Anasazi lacked milk and eggs, which are important in everybody's diet. We know the Indians missed the calcium the milk and eggs would have supplied because some of them had poor teeth. As soon as the Indians of the pueblos learned about cows and chickens, they began using milk and eggs. Then their teeth improved, for their diet was perfect.

ALL IN THE COURSE
OF A LIFETIME

THE ANASAZI were usually quiet people, who liked to have things calm and orderly around them. These Indians did not get upset about things that went wrong, and they thought it was rude to speak loudly or move quickly or to want to own more and better things than other people had. People learned, from the time that they were little children, to be considerate of others, to be polite, to share, and to take part in the actions of the whole group.

Because the Anasazi were considerate of each other, they were able to live pleasantly together in cities, and to develop their arts and crafts. They could have great religious ceremonies because each person was willing to take part. The Anasazi were able to farm and to divide their scanty water supply fairly because they could meet and talk over their problems and work out a solution together.

When an Anasazi baby was born, his mother's mother was there to take care of him. Grandmother washed the new baby with yucca suds. Then she coated him with deer's grease, for she had no olive oil or mineral oil to use as a modern hospital does. Then Grandmother wrapped the baby in a blanket and carried him into the living room to meet his aunts. (His mother's and father's sisters, and their women cousins, were all called aunts.)

Probably some of the aunts talked Indian baby talk to the new member of the family. Then, when the child had met the first of its human relations, Grandmother carried the baby outdoors to meet the world.

This was the baby's first ceremony, and naturally it was a naming ceremony. Before the newborn was born, Grandmother prepared a Corn Mother for it. She chose a perfect ear of white corn, with the rows and kernels completely filled and evenly spaced. She stripped the husks back from the ear and cleaned off the silk. She fastened a tuft of white eagle down—the Anasazi called it a breath feather because a breath would stir it—to the top of the ear of corn, as if it were a dancer's headdress. The Corn Mother was ready ahead of time, waiting for the baby to be born. As soon as the infant was dressed, Grandmother passed the Corn Mother four times up and down its body, and as she did so, she told the baby its name.

Next Grandmother picked the baby up and carried it onto the roof of its mother's house. She held the newborn out to the east, to the south, to the west, and to the north, as far as her arms could reach. She introduced it to the universe by telling the four corners of the world its name. If the baby were a boy, perhaps she named him Juniper Stands Tall or Brush Where the Deer Hides. If the baby were a girl, she might have a name like Rain Clouds Blossoming or Corn Tassels Swaying. As she named the baby, Grandmother asked for the blessing of all the spirits of the sky and earth:

PRAYER SPOKEN WHILE PRESENTING AN INFANT
TO THE SUN

Now this is the day.
Our child,
Into the daylight you will go out standing.
Preparing for your day,

We have passed our days.
When all your days were at an end,
When eight days were passed,
Our sun father
Went in to sit down at his sacred place.
And our night fathers,
Having come out standing to their sacred place,
Our sun father,
Having come out standing to his sacred place,
Our child, it is your day.
This day,
The flesh of the white corn, prayer meal,
To our sun father
This prayer meal we offer.
May your road be fulfilled.
Reaching to the road of your sun father,
When your road is fulfilled,
In your thoughts may we live,
May we be the ones your thoughts will embrace,
For this, on this day,
To our sun father,
We offer prayer meal.
To this end:
May you help us all to finish our roads.

For the first four days after the baby was born, the child's father and brothers stayed away from home, and only women were allowed in the mother's house. Grandmother carried the baby outside to meet its father. Often most of the women of the family stayed all four days, cooking and making baskets, talking and singing. It was a party for them, and their husbands

Grandmother Holding a Newborn

had to wait for them to come home.

When the baby was four days old, its father and brothers could come home, and the aunts returned to their own houses. The family life settled down to normal again.

The Anasazi used two kinds of cradles. One was a carrying cradle, similar to the ones other Indian groups used, but with a basketry frame. Probably Grandmother made it, and perhaps while she worked on the cradle before the baby was born, she thought about names and decided on one.

What is believed to be the oldest Anasazi cradle found so far, and is about one thousand years old, is made with a foundation of two oval willow rings. The rings were tied together, one above the other, and strips of juniper were laid across between them. This mat was the bed on which the baby was laid, and to which it was bound with strips of soft deerskin or cotton cloth.

In some Anasazi graves babies have been found still wrapped in the cotton and fur blankets their grandfathers or fathers had made for them. Often the lower end of the wrapping blanket was in two parts, so it would be easy to change the baby's rabbit-fur diaper without undressing it. The mother tied the soft rabbit fur, or deerskin, and milkweed pads in

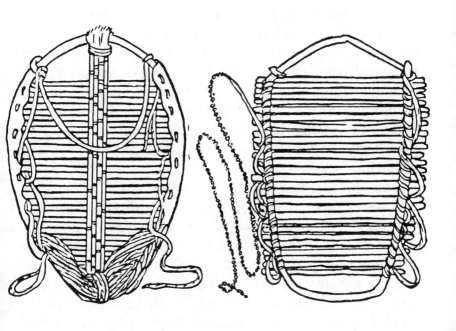

TWO OF THE OLDEST INDIAN CRADLES-ABOUT 1,000 YRS. OLD

place with deerskin bandages, for she had no safety pins.

Probably the Anasazi mothers used the flat carrying cradles only when they were going out to gather food and had to take their babies with them. Otherwise, like modern Pueblo Indian women, a mother usually put the baby in a hammock. She made a hammock cradle by hanging ropes from the living room rafters and stretching a blanket across the space between the ropes. She laid the baby on the blanket and tied it in place so it wouldn't fall out. One of the regular jobs of the older children in a Pueblo Indian family is swinging the baby in its hammock cradle.

As the little children grew up and began to walk, they learned to do small tasks around the house. Even the smallest boy could carry a few chips or little sticks for his mother's cooking fire. A tiny girl would have her own little water jar or carrying basket, so she could help her mother bring in supplies.

The children had plenty of time to play, and nobody expected them to work hard, or for too long at a time. Both the boys and girls played tag. They had balls made of deerskin stuffed with wads of yucca leaves, and they played kickball and shinny. The boys tied flat sticks to rawhide or sinew strings and whirled their bull-roarers around their heads to make a thundering noise and frighten the girls. The children played with whiptops, made of wood and spun with long strips of rawhide cord.

The boys also had small rabbit sticks and atlatls and darts or bows and arrows. They practiced shooting and learned how to hunt as soon as they were old enough to hold their weapons.

The girls must have played house a lot, judging from the amount of toy pottery they made, or their mothers and aunts made for them. The little girls had rag dolls, and dolls that were made of ears of corn, and dolls that were made of stuffed squirrel or gopher skins. The girls played cat's cradle, too, with yucca or cotton strings their fathers spun for them.

In the spring each Indian town had a series of races and shinny games across the cornfields and gardens before the crops were planted. First, the smallest children raced, then those who were a little older, next the twelve and thirteen year olds, and then the young men and women. Last of all was the race for the oldest people. The Indians believed that as each group ran a little faster and a little harder than the one before it, the corn would see that it was supposed to grow tall and

Entrance to a Kiva

ripen to maturity as people did.

Even in our own times, an Indian child who is four or five years old probably notices that his father is away from home almost every day and sometimes is gone overnight. Perhaps when a little boy asks where his father is, he is told that the men are all out hunting, or are in the cornfields, or have gone to the kiva. Indian boys must grow up knowing that kivas are special, sacred places and that grown men spend a great deal of time in them.

One morning, when a boy was six or seven, his Indian father took him to the kiva, too. They walked across the plaza to the kiva roof and across that to the entrance hatchway. They went down the ladder, with one tall pole projecting high above the roof, and one shorter pole. At the bottom of the ladder they stood on the floor of an underground room with painted walls.

On ordinary days, the kiva must have looked more like a workshop than a sacred place. Some men sat around chipping out stone points. Others rubbed down arrow or dart shafts with pieces of sandstone, or twisted sinew strings together, or bound feathers in place on their shafts. Some men had spindles and were spinning cotton thread or dogs' hair yarn. Others had given their wives haircuts and were braiding ropes. And one or two men sat with their backs to the others, facing their looms, which were fastened to beams set in the walls or the ceiling of the kiva.

Behind the ladder, between it and the wall, where no one would enter it irreverently, was the sacred part of the kiva. Probably the father warned his little boy not to go near the shrine, or to disturb the older men who went there to pray or meditate. And the father certainly showed his son where the family work space was located in the kiva and told him to stay there, or close by, and not to bother other people.

While the younger men worked in the kiva, one of the older ones told stories. Maybe he explained about the paintings on the walls. He told why there was a picture of the Sun God, and what the paintings of the rain clouds and their spirits meant, with the mountains painted above them and growing corn to represent the cornfields painted below. These explanations and stories were really lessons, and the boys gathered around the teller of tales were learning the ways and beliefs of their people just as if they were in school.

As time went on, the boy spent more and more time in the kiva with the men, when he was not working with them in the fields. In some Anasazi groups it was the custom for a man to take his sister's sons—his nephews—into his kiva, for they belonged to his clan and family and not to their father's. In whatever kiva a boy was trained, he learned the stories of his ancestors, from the time of their long journey from the north to the country of the Four Corners. He learned the songs the oldest men sang as they traveled, and the songs their descendants sang as they worked in the fields or at their crafts.

With the songs, the boy learned the dances and ceremonies that expressed the religious beliefs of his people. He was taught to be clean: to bathe often in the creeks or springs and to wash his hair with yucca suds before each ceremony. He learned to make his own clothes and to exchange his work for things other people had made. He was taught everything a man needed to know.

When both boys and girls were about twelve years old, they were shown the masks, representing the gods, which the

Interior of a Kiva

dancers wore in certain ceremonies. Before they were initiated, though, the children were punished for all the bad things they had ever done by being whipped with yucca bundles. The whipping hurt enough to be remembered all their lives long. Even when they were very small, children knew that a time would come when they would be called out before the whole town, and all their misdeeds would be recited. The fact that everybody would hear, and that people would laugh at them, frightened the children more than the whipping. For that reason, Indian children were generally well behaved, so that they would get off lightly when the time for public punishment came. At the time of their initiations, children were always given new names. If they had been good, the names were pleasant ones; but if they had been bad, the names would be funny. The fear of getting a bad name was another thing that made the children well behaved.

All his life an Anasazi man spent more time in his kiva than in any other one place. If he were not farming or hunting, he went to the kiva to work, just as men now go to their offices or shops. Sometimes the men did not go home to eat; they waited for their wives or mothers or sisters to bring food to the kiva entrance. Then the men carried the dishes inside and ate their meals while they worked. Afterward they set the dishes outside the door on the roof for the women to take home. Only when there was a big, important ceremony, in which they were required to take part or which they were given special permission to watch, did the women enter the kivas.

While their brothers went to school in the kivas—it was like boarding school, for after they were ten years old the boys often slept there with one of the old men to watch them. Meanwhile the girls were having home economics lessons at home. They learned to make baskets and to shape and fire pottery. Most important of all, they learned to grind corn and to cook.

Little girls were taught to break up the grains of corn on the coarse metate. At first the children probably used one end of the mano and cracked the grains of corn like nuts, one at

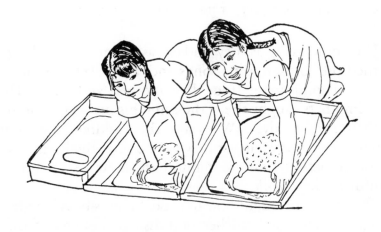

Women Grinding Corn

a time. Later, the girls got used to holding their stones properly and learned to break up several grains at a time.

Each day a girl worked at the metates. As she grew older, she learned to grind finer and finer meal. And as she grew older, she spent more time in the kitchen and ground more meal each time. When she was eighteen or nineteen, her family expected her to be able to grind all day without stopping, and to turn out meal that was as fine as dust. When she could do that, a girl was considered ready to get married.

Another chore that the girls did was to carry water for the family. They learned to balance their water jars on their heads, their arms swinging at their sides or loaded with firewood, and not spill a drop. The water jars were made with little cups in their bases, to fit on the tops of the girls' heads; but even so, when they were filled they were heavy and hard to carry. Little girls had little jars that held about a cupful at a time and went with their mothers and older sisters, or with their aunts, to bring water for the house. If the mother was replastering her walls, or the father was mixing adobe to build a new room, the girls carried all the water that was used in building. At Acoma Pueblo the women used to go up and down a hundred-foot ladder cut in the rock with jars of water on their heads.

The women sang as they worked, as the men did. The girls learned the corn-grinding songs and the basket-making and pottery-shaping songs from their mothers and aunts. Their grandmothers taught them the same history songs the boys learned in the kivas. Wherever the children and young people were, and whatever they were doing, there was always an older person near, to remind them to be careful and skillful in their work.

The girls were taught how to make brooms by tying grasses or yucca leaves or branches of brush or boughs of piñon together. Every good housekeeper had several brooms. She had a very small one to brush up the ashes on the hearth and a larger one to sweep the floor. There was a long-handled, flexible one to clean the rafters and a short, stubby one to get dirt out of the cracks in the storeroom floor. And there was another, a specially heavy broom, to sweep the ground in the plaza right in front of the house.

A young man began to make his wife's wedding dress long before he decided who she was going to be. He spun miles of white cotton thread, and from it he wove her a white one-piece dress and a fine white cotton shawl. He made heavier thread and braided a wide white sash with its long, braided fringe looped around balls of cornhusk. He made her high-topped, black-soled moccasin boots. He made a case of fine yucca matting to hold the whole outfit, and if he did not know how to make jewelry he traded some of his spinning or weaving for a necklace and bracelets for his bride to wear. He started work on the wedding costume when he was about fourteen and worked on it until he finished it, which was usually when he was about twenty. In fact, a young man was not allowed to marry until he had provided clothes for his wife. If he could not spin or weave well but was a good farmer or weaponmaker, he was allowed to trade his work to a weaver, who would make the wedding outfit.

Of course long before the dress was finished the young man had decided who was going to wear it. By that time he knew the girls in his town and knew he could not marry the ones who belonged to his clan, for they were considered his close relations. He might dance with some girl from another clan during a ceremony, and afterward watch her work with her mother and sisters, and perhaps help her carry water from the spring for her family. Little by little, the young people became acquainted. It was against the rules for them to be alone together before they married.

Sometimes the young men played on their flutes or sang serenades to the girls they wanted to marry. Here is a love song that is still sung at Santa Clara Pueblo:

THE WILLOWS BY THE WATERSIDE

My little breath, under the willows by the waterside
  we used to sit,
And there the yellow cottonwood bird came and sang.
That I remember and therefore I weep.
Under the growing corn we used to sit,
And there the little leaf bird came and sang.
That I remember, and therefore I weep.
There on the meadow of yellow flowers we used to walk.
Oh, my little breath! Oh, my little heart!
There on the meadow of blue flowers we used to walk.
Alas! How long ago we two walked in that pleasant way.
Then everything was happy, but alas! How long ago.
There on the meadow of crimson flowers we used to walk.
Oh, my little breath, now I go there alone in sorrow.

In some pueblos even today, and in all of them as late as the early 1900s, when the young man and woman had made up their minds the boy went to his parents and told them he wanted to be engaged. They talked to him seriously, for they wanted to be sure he understood how important marriage is. When the mother and father were certain their son had made up his mind, they went to visit the parents of the girl.

Of course the girl had talked to her parents by that time, so her mother and father expected the boy's family to call. When the visitors first came in and sat down, they talked about the weather, and the corn crop, and how the beans were growing, and the chances of going rabbit hunting for quite a long time before they got around to talking about marriage. It would not have been polite to start right in with the main subject.

Even when the parents did begin to talk about it, they were very careful how they spoke. They explained that their son was a nice young man and a hard worker. They told how much land he had of his own and how well his corn grew. They said he was even industrious enough to take care of a wife, and they wondered if such a fine girl as the other family's daughter would be willing to marry him.

The girl's family answered by saying that she, too, was a hard worker and could grind corn all day without getting tired. She could carry plenty of water, too, and she was a good cook. She really ought to get married and start raising a family of her own, for her mother had already given her a little house. Naturally, they had hoped that a really fine young man, like the other parents' son, would want to marry her.

Then the girl's parents called her in from the next room, where she could probably hear everything that was said, and the boy's father and mother beckoned to him to come in from outside the house. The parents took turns explaining to the young people that they had all agreed, and that they were all very happy, and that they hoped their children would be happy, too. The young people thanked their parents for giving them permission to marry and promised to try to make a happy and peaceful home for the older people to visit.

Next, the girl prepared a present for her mother-in-law. She ground fine cornmeal, to show that she was able to keep house by herself. No one was allowed to help a girl with this work. She must do it all alone, and she must make as much meal as she could—at least four big baskets full. If she made only a little, or if the meal was coarse, people would laugh at her and say that she was not ready to marry.

When the meal was ground as fine as it could be, the girl and her parents put on their best clothes. They gathered together presents of baskets, pottery, clothes, and jewelry, and they went in a little procession, with the girl walking ahead, to the boy's mother's house. They carried their gifts into the living room and laid them on the floor before the boy's parents. Everybody in the house looked at the presents and praised them and thanked the givers. The boy's mother inspected the meal, and told her new daughter how skillful she was and thanked her. Then the boy's family served a feast, and the girl went home with her mother and father.

The next day, the boy brought the girl her wedding clothes. His mother and father brought presents to the girl's parents. Everyone looked at the wedding clothes and admired the beautiful work that had gone into them. Then they all had another feast, and the boy and his parents went home.

For the next four days all the women in the girl's family cooked and ground cornmeal and ground cornmeal and cooked. They were getting ready for the big feast. The family sent word to everybody in their own town, and in nearby towns, to invite people to come to the wedding. Visitors came and stayed and visited with their friends, and helped with the preparations.

On the wedding day, the girl's female relatives washed her hair early in the morning and combed it dry and smooth. Then they dressed her in her lovely new white dress and draped her shawl over her loose, hanging hair so that her face was hidden. They bound her new white moccasins on her feet and wrapped her white deerskin leggings on her legs. Then they led her into the room where all the relatives, friends, and guests of both families had gathered.

The boy came in, wearing fine new clothes, and his parents followed him. The head priest of the village joined the hands of the young people and prayed that they might be given long life and great happiness. He gave them a pottery jug with

A Pueblo Wedding

two spouts, so each of them could drink a sip of the same herb-scented water. The priest talked seriously to the young people and instructed them how to behave.

Then the young couple were given a flat basket that held cornmeal mush. The girl drew a cross on the surface of the mush with her forefinger, from one edge of the basket to the other. She sprinkled corn pollen along the lines of the cross. Then each dipped up a finger-load of mush and ate it. They were supposed to eat the whole basketful without any salt or seasoning, as their first meal together.

When the ceremonial meal was finished, the girl's sisters lifted the shawl off her head and laid it around her shoulders. They dressed her hair, drawing it back to the nape of her neck and folding it into a bundle, as all married women wore their hair.

Then the older women brought in the rest of the wedding feast. They served the young couple first, then the head priest, then the parents of the newlyweds. After that the big feast of dried meat, parched corn, tamales, *piki*, and fruit with honey, as well as other good things, was served to everybody. After they ate dinner, the girl's parents gave a feast, which everybody attended.

At the end of the feast, the young people went home to the bride's own house, where they lived from that time on. If they had a family, and needed more rooms, they asked the town council for permission to build a new room on the house. If they needed more land to feed their growing family, the man asked the council to assign him the use of another field. Sometimes a man was lucky and was granted a field near the one he had already cultivated. Sometimes he had to be satisfied with a field a long way from the one he owned. Then he had to work harder and travel farther from home to be able to raise his crop.

As the family grew up, the parents trained and taught their children as they had been taught themselves. They talked to the children and tried to show them how to be polite and respectful. Perhaps on winter evenings they sent a child to invite the members of a neighboring family to come and visit them. Then everybody sat by the fire and told what they called "the little stories," stories that were like our fairy tales. True histories and serious stories were told in the kivas, and only the little stories were supposed to be told at home. Even the little stories could only be told when the crops were gathered in and the year's work was finished. When the first snow had fallen and three bright stars stood clear together in mid-sky at midnight, the old people said the time had come to tell the little stories.

While they listened to the little stories, the children ate sunflower seeds or dried berries. They cracked piñon nuts and sometimes popped corn to eat while they listened. At the end of the evening of storytelling, the company went home, and the children were put to bed.

Generally, people were very happy after they married, but once in a great while, for some reason, a man and woman would fail to get along well. If the man were unhappy, he could take his clothes and weapons to his mother's house or his sister's home, or go to the kiva to stay. If the woman were unhappy or dissatisfied, she could put her husband's possessions on the ground outside the door of the house. Then he had to gather them up and go to live with his own family. After that, the two people were divorced, and after a summer and winter had gone by either of them who wanted to could marry somebody else. If they had children, the children stayed with the mother because they belonged to her family and clan.

Among the Anasazi, older people were always treated with great respect. Their advice was listened to and followed, and they were given all the food and clothes they needed. No one expected old people to do physical work unless they wanted to. Younger people thought the old ones had earned a rest, and that the advice and comfort they could give others were worth more than weaving or hunting or grinding corn.

When people died, their bodies were buried with great respect, and with many prayers that the spirits would welcome them and receive them into a new life. Their Corn Mothers, which had hung from the rafters of their houses all through their lives, were wrapped in embroidered cloth and placed in their hands, to accompany their spirits to the afterworld.

Sometimes people were buried in or near their homes, and sometimes they were buried on the mountainsides. Anasazi customs about funerals changed a number of times during the centuries. In some of the greatest Indian cities the people must have been afraid of the dead, for their cemeteries have never been found. At other times and places, as we know, the spirits were loved and respected, and the bodies that had held them were kept as near home as possible.

Lives of people, as the Anasazi said, come and go with the growing seasons, like the lives of plants. It is important for everybody to live in the right way, to be kind and polite and respectful, so that others will see that they have raised a good crop in their minds and hearts, as well as in their fields.

RELIGION, GOVERNMENT, AND HEALING

NOW WE COME to certain parts of Indian life that outsiders have been told very little about. We know what
the Indians made, and what their tools and houses and
clothes were like. We know how modern Indians make and
do most things in their everyday lives. But religion and government and medicine are serious, important things. No one
Indian today knows all about them in his own town, and he
does not like to explain the portion he does know to strangers.
We must put together what we see, and the little our Indian
friends are allowed to tell us, to know even a part of the rules
by which the modern Indians live. Probably no non-Indian
will ever know all these rules.

We do know that from the earliest town-building times to
the present, the government and religion of the Anasazi and
their descendants have been closely related. We know, too,
that both have always centered around the kivas. We are told
that each Indian town has always been governed by its religious
leader, with the help of a council. And we know an Aztec
Indian word, *cacique* (cah-SEE-kay), that can be used to
describe the religious chief of an Indian pueblo.

Very few outsiders know who the *cacique* of any pueblo is.
Each *cacique* has a group of assistants, and these are the men

non-Indians meet. Each pueblo has a governor; he has a very important position among his people. The governor talks to visitors and tells them whether they may walk in the plaza of the pueblo and visit the Indian homes, or whether they are not allowed to stay on a particular day. The governor tells the visitors where they may park their cars, where they may sit or stand to watch the Indians dancing, and whether or not they may take photographs. The governor also talks to official visitors and writes letters on town business. The governor is elected by the other members of the pueblo, and probably each election has to be approved by the *cacique* of the town.

The governors of the pueblos have assistants in administering business matters. There is usually a lieutenant governor and a war chief, or assistant, in each pueblo. They carry out the directions of the governor, and they also have separate duties of their own, which vary so much from town to town that it is hard to describe them accurately. There is a town crier, or announcer, in each pueblo. His job is to tell the people what the council has decided: whether it is time to plant the corn, when a particular dance will be held, and who is to take part in a ceremony.

The Pueblo Indian families share in town government, although we do not know exactly how important their share is. We do know that the families have a very important place in religion.

The families we are talking about now are not simple small families of mother and father and children. They are big families, and they *extend* far enough to include all the people in the pueblo who claim to be descended from a single person. Widely extended families of that sort are called *clans*. Usually their members all have the same last name and call themselves one people. Clans are found all over the world, in Australia and Central Africa, as well as in Scotland and Ireland and among the Indians of the Southwest.

The Anasazi clan names were taken from plants, animals, or precious objects. There are Deer People and Squash People and Turtle People and Bean People. In some pueblos there are Turquoise People and Shell People and Snake People. Perhaps these names came from the Old Ancestors, or perhaps they were intended to show where the clan had originally lived.

In each pueblo the clans are divided into two groups. Half the people of each town are known as the Winter People. They live on the north side of the town plaza. The other half live on the south side and are called the Summer People. In most pueblos a man belongs to the same clan, and the same group of clans, as his mother. In a few Indian towns, though, people are said to be born into their fathers' families.

Usually each clan has its own kiva, where the men can go to work or talk and hold small ceremonies. On each side of the pueblo there is a larger kiva, one for the Winter People and one for the Summer People. These two main kivas are used for more important ceremonies, where large crowds of people participate or watch. In some Indian towns there is another big, main kiva, where everybody goes for certain ceremonies.

Each clan has priests, who help the *cacique*. Sometimes each clan sends a representative to the governor's advisory council. As far as we know, the representatives are always men. There are certain women who hold religious positions in each pueblo, but the Indians have never told anybody very much about their duties.

In all their religious activities, the Indians do things four times. They speak of the world as having four quarters, or sections, and they say that a human life has four divisions: childhood, youth, maturity, and old age. There are four seasons of the year and four main divisions of the day and night. It seems as if the Indians themselves might have willed that four states should meet in the heart of their old country, and that the area should be known as the Four Corners.

The Pueblo Indians believe that everything has a spirit: stones, mountains, streams, fish, birds, animals, and plants, as well as humans. They honor these spirits and give dances for them. The spirits of the Sun, Rain, Clouds, Snow, Moon, and Earth are the greatest of all the spirits. We do not know for certain whether or not the Pueblo Indians worship a Power Beyond the Spirits. Some non-Indians who have lived with the Indians for a long time and have studied their ways closely believe that they do.

When the Spaniards came into the Southwest, they taught the Indians about the Christian God and the saints, for the Spaniards were Catholics. The Indians were baptized, and a church was built in every pueblo. None of the kivas was permanently destroyed, however, and the Indians continued to worship in their old ways at the same time that they attended services in the churches. It seemed as if the Indians thought the new God was another spirit, or perhaps that he was the Power Beyond the Spirits that they had always known. Today the Pueblo Indians both attend church and hold kiva ceremonies, as their ancestors did.

Because the Indians had to do so much hard work to get food, their most important ceremonies were concerned with hunting and bringing rain. The Pueblo Indians believe that by imitating the actions of animals or plants, they can encourage the plants to grow or the animals to allow the hunters to approach. So their ceremonies take the form of dances: hunting dances, planting dances, rain dances, and dances of thanksgiving for good harvests. Sometimes the dancers wear masks to identify them more closely with the spirits they represent. Some people take part in the dances, and others watch. The watchers receive as much of the blessing of the nature spirits as the dancers do, for the Indians believe that a ceremony is incomplete without somebody to watch it. If visitors come to a dance and look on quietly and respectfully, then they, too, can receive the blessing of the spirits.

That is why it is possible to describe some parts of the ceremonies. Outsiders are forbidden to enter the kivas, or stand on them, or even come too close to them. But visitors may watch the dancers in the plazas and see the outdoor parts of the ceremonies.

On the twenty-third of January, the Indians at San Ildefonso Pueblo hold their annual hunting dance. The weather is cold at that time of year, and often there is snow on the ground. This is the season when deer and elk come down from the mountains to the gardens near the houses, and paw aside the snow covering the stubble in the cornfields, looking for something to eat. It is the time when supplies from the last harvest run low, and when meat and fat are necessary parts of the Indians' diet.

The dancers spend the four days and nights before the main ceremony in the kiva. Their relatives bring them food and water, and leave it outside the kiva door. Those inside pray and practice their songs and dances until they are ready to perform the ceremony. All the women clean house and cook in preparation for the celebration.

Early in the dark morning, watchers gather outside the pueblo and watch the hills to the east. As the sun begins to bleach the sky, the watchers see a cloud of smoke rise from a fire on the southern hill. They hear sharp, quick calls, like those of animals. As the light and cold grow more intense, the watchers shiver and pray.

Then, down the hill, hidden by a cloud of smoke until they are almost on top of the audience, come the dancers. They are led by a woman, wearing an old-fashioned Pueblo dress, and barefoot. Her hair streams down her back, and her face is painted with red disks on her forehead, cheekbones, and chin. In her hands the woman carries spruce boughs, which she waves before her face.

A group of men gather around a drum, a little away from the audience, and sing to draw the woman spirit and the animal spirits closer to the village.

The animal dancers follow the woman. They are men, wearing white shirts and white kilts embroidered or painted with water snake or other clan designs. Their feet are bare. Each man has a fox skin tied to the back of his belt, and each man wears a headdress. There is a visor, or half-mask, across his black-painted face, to hide his human features. On his head he wears horns or antlers carved from wood to show what animal he represents. Sometimes there are deer and antelope,

Hunting Dance at San Ildefonso Pueblo

mountain sheep, and buffalo dancers. Sometimes there are only antelope and deer. Each dancer carries a cane in either hand and leans on them as he dances. The canes represent the forelegs of the animal.

Usually there are little boys in the dance group, dressed like the men except that they wear yellow capes over their shoulders. They represent the little deer and antelope fawns.

Behind the animal dancers come the two hunters, each with his face painted red. Each man wears his best clothes, and his hair hangs loose over his shoulders. Each hunter holds a miniature bow and arrows. They follow the animal dancers, who pretend not to see them.

When the dancers reach the outskirts of the pueblo, they stop to dance. The hunters pretend to shoot at the animal dancers, and the dancers turn and twist to escape the arrows. The woman dances to one side, while the hunting dance is performed. Then she leads the men into the plaza. The group dances four times—once on each side of the square plaza. By that time full daylight has come. The dancers and drummers go into the kiva, and the other people go to their homes for breakfast.

There is a service in the church at midmorning, and everybody except the dancers is expected to be present. After the service the dancers come out of the kiva and dance again in the plaza. They dance four or eight times at intervals during the day, and late in the afternoon they return to the kiva for the last time. The hunting dance is over for that year.

One of the greatest and most important of Pueblo Indian ceremonies is called the Corn Dance. Every Indian pueblo holds one Corn Dance each summer; some of them have two or three. The dates are set in some secret way that has not been explained to outsiders, and they vary a great deal. Jemez Pueblo has its Corn Dance as late as the twelfth of November.

The earliest one held each spring is at San Felipe Pueblo and it is given on May Day. San Felipe is one of the largest pueblos. The town has changed very little since it was built in 1725. Its houses still stand wall to wall on each of the four sides of the main plaza. There is a narrow passage into the plaza between the houses at each corner of the town, and outside the main plaza there are several smaller ones, each built around a kiva. The ground level in the main plaza is about four feet lower than the walk in front of the houses all around it.

Everybody in town who is able to dance is expected to take part in the Corn Dance. The rest drum or sing for the dancers, or cook for them and for the visitors who come to the pueblo on that day. The *cacique* and his assistants probably assign their duties to the people. There are four days and nights of preparation, when the dancers spend most of their time in the kiva, learning songs, practicing steps, and praying that they may do the dance properly and bring rain to the crops.

Early in the morning, the dancers come out of the kivas, and everybody goes to the church. There they pray and are blessed. After the service, some of the older men take the figures of the saints from the altar and carry them to the plaza. They set them in a leafy arbor that has been built of branches and hung with beautiful blankets and embroideries. It is at the north end of the plaza. The saints are there to watch and enjoy the dance, like the other spirits who have been invited to attend during the days of preparation in the kiva. Some of the old men sit on benches just outside the arbor, to keep the saints company, and to see that nobody does anything disrespectful to them. The saints are the invited guests of the Indian spirits and must be treated courteously.

When the saints and their guardians are settled and everything is ready, the drums in one of the kivas begin to beat, and the sound is like thunder coming from underground. Then the Summer People enter the plaza. They make two long lines, from east to west, across the middle of the open space. The most active people are at the heads of the lines, and the grandparents and little children at the foot. The youngest children are four or five years old, and they are called "The Little Tails." The Indians have a saying that "Everybody has been a Little

Tail," which means, "All people are pretty much alike."

Everybody is dressed in dancing costume. The women and girls wear their hair hanging loose and long down their backs, like water pouring over rocks. They wear the old-fashioned Anasazi dresses, made of a piece of hand-woven dark blue cloth, usually wool. The dress is fastened over the right shoulder and under the left arm, and is held in place with silver brooches. Each woman wears an upright wooden tablet, with her clan symbol carved and painted on it, tied to the top of her head. She is barefoot and carries blue spruce branches in her hands. She wears turquoise or silver earrings, and all the rings and necklaces and bracelets she owns. Her face is painted—yellow if she belongs to the Summer People, blue if she is on the Winter side of the pueblo.

The men, too, let their hair hang loose and long. Young me, who have cut their hair sometimes wear long horsehair wigs. Each man has a bunch of red and yellow and orange macaw feathers tied to the crown of his head. Each man is bare above the waist, but his body is painted yellow or blue, according to his group. Around their upper arms, the men wear painted leather bands, with spruce branches thrust through them. Each man carries a gourd rattle in his right hand and spruce boughs in his left. Around his waist each man wears a kilt of hand-woven, white cotton cloth, embroidered or painted with his clan symbol or with a water-snake design. His kilt is held by a wide plaited sash of white cotton string, with long fringed and tasseled ends hanging to the ground. These belts are called rain sashes, and when the men dance the fringes shake up and down and look like falling water. Tied to his kilt in back, and hanging down over his rain sash, the man wears a fox or coyote skin. He has on high-topped, buckskin moccasins and has strips of skunk fur tied around his ankles. Each man wears earrings and rings and a necklace with a pendant made of an inlaid shell.

A chorus of men follows the dancers. Usually the singers are older men, but sometimes young ones who are especially good singers are invited to join the chorus. One man carries a huge drum made of a cottonwood trunk. The drum is so large and heavy it has a foot so the man can rest it on the ground while he beats the drumhead. The singers and the drummer wear bright-colored cotton shirts and tight white trousers, like pajama trousers. They tie their hair in tight bunches at the backs of their necks with strips of hand-woven woolen cloth. The musicians wear handmade silver belts and many necklaces and bracelets and rings. Usually the older men wear earrings.

One man in the chorus carries a long, heavy pole, with a narrow banner tied along it from the top almost to the bottom. The top of the pole is decorated with a bunch of long, brightly colored macaw feathers, and the banner is embroidered with rain symbols. No non-Indian really knows what the banner means. No Pueblo Indian has ever been willing to tell what it stands for. The man who carries it stands behind the dancers and slowly waves the pole back and forth, from side to side above their heads.

When all the Summer People have filed into the plaza, the dancing begins. At first the lines of dancers move slowly, facing one another, back and forth and from side to side. Then the drumbeat quickens, and the singing grows louder. The dancing becomes faster and more complicated. The lines of people begin to make patterns in the plaza: short lines and long ones, and squares and oblongs, to represent the pueblo and its fields. They make moving, merging circles to represent raindrops and streams and the patterns they make on the earth.

On either side of the dancers there is a group of Indian police, called *koshari* (koe-SHAH-ree). They are there to keep order in the audience and to help the dancers. If someone's costume is loosened by his movements, or a string of beads breaks, or a moccasin string is untied, a *koshari* comes to repair the damage. The dancer never stops moving while the *koshari* is busy helping him, for the *koshari* represent invisible spirits. The dancers always pretend that the *koshari* are not there.

At the end of four songs, the Summer People leave the plaza, and the Winter People dance in their turn. They have their own chorus and drummer and standard-bearer and *koshari*, and they sing and dance while the Summer People rest in their kiva. When the Winter People have finished their four songs, the Summer People return to the plaza.

The dancing goes on all day until late in the afternoon. If there is rain, the people dance more happily, for they believe that their dancing brought the rainfall. When the late light grows level across the plaza, the dance ends. Both groups of people meet in the plaza for the last dance of the day. Then they all file out and return to the church for a blessing. The old men who have kept the saints company all day take the figures home and see that they are safely indoors and settled for the night. The *koshari* make one last trip around the plaza, beating a small hand drum, to tell the people that the dance is over, and to make sure nothing has been lost or forgotten and that all the visitors have gone home. That night there is a great feast in every house in the pueblo.

Here is a Corn Dance Song, from Zuni Pueblo. There are probably hundreds of songs like it, and each pueblo has its own.

Corn Dance Song

Who, ah, know ye who—
Who, ah, know ye who—
Who was it made a picture the first?
It was the bright Rainbow Youth,
    Rainbow Youth—
Ay, behold, it was even thus—
        Clouds came,
        And rain came,
        Close following—
Rainbow then colored all!

There are many other religious dances given in the modern pueblos. The Hopi Snake Dance, in which the priests hold live rattlesnakes, and the Kachina Dances are very famous. So is the house-blessing Shalako Dance given at Zuni Pueblo. In the Kachina Dances dolls dressed to represent the spirits and the dancers are given to the girls, and toy bows and arrows are given to the boys. In nearly all pueblos give-away dances are held at different times during the year.

Usually Indian dancers wear their Corn Dance costumes for other dances, and add special accessories for each ceremony. In the Hopi Butterfly or Rainbow Dance, the women wear rain sashes, and the men have red scarfs tied diagonally across their chests. The men and women dance in couples, and each pair holds a Rainbow Staff between them.

We have been told that the Pueblo Indians have healing ceremonies and dances. These are very often held in the kivas. A few non-Indians have been treated by Indian doctors, but they have been made to promise never to tell what was done to help them.

We also know that often parents promise that if their children are cured of sickness they themselves, or the children, will take part in a particular dance. But all these cures are concerned with religion, and therefore the Indians keep them very secret.

However, every Pueblo Indian mother and grandmother knows how to take care of small sicknesses in her family. They tie spiderwebs or cobwebs over cuts, to make the blood coagulate. They give doses of herb teas for stomachaches and colds. One Pueblo Indian remedy for a cold is to tie an old, worn stocking filled with cooked chile peppers around the sick person's throat, and to make him eat a big dish of chile. The chile is so hot it cooks the sickness right out!

The worst sicknesses that the Anasazi had were in their teeth and bones, as the result of not having milk and eggs. In some of the skulls that have been taken from Anasazi houses, the teeth were splintered and blackened and worn down to the jawbones. Those people must have had terrible toothaches!

Corn Dance

Probably all they could do at home to ease the pain was drink hot water and herb tea, so they must have spent a lot of time in the kiva, praying to be relieved of their suffering.

After the Spaniards brought cows and chickens to the Southwest, and the Indian children had milk and eggs to eat, these conditions improved. In recent times, nobody has had to knock a tooth out of an Indian's mouth to release the evil spirit that is hurting the person. Nowadays most Pueblo Indians have very good teeth, and would be greatly surprised if they learned what painful toothaches their ancestors had to endure.

THE TIME OF THE GREAT CHANGES

T HE ANASAZI lived in the Four Corners, while they developed from roving hunters and gatherers to planters and basketmakers, and then into cliff-dwelling potters and priests and farmers who built cities and lived comfortably and well. The Indians worked hard, but they had learned that each person's work meant most when it benefited others. The Anasazi were prosperous and happy, and they were generally peaceful.

Once in a while their quiet life was interrupted. Away in the Northwest, in country the Anasazi had traveled through on their way south from Alaska, were later emigrants who probably had come from another part of Asia. These people were hunters and fighters who lived in roving bands. They called themselves *Dene* (day-NAY), which is another Indian name that means "people." We call them Athapascans and divide them into several large groups, including the different kinds of Apaches and the Navajos.

The early Athapascans raided other peoples for supplies of seeds and dried fruits and buckskins and meat. After the Athapascans discovered the great cities of the Four Corners, and the supplies of corn and beans and squash and beautiful textiles of the Anasazi, they raided the Indian towns more and more often. Each time the Athapascans attacked an Anasazi city they carried off food and clothing and some of the Anasazi people themselves. They wanted slaves, as well as any property they could seize. They destroyed the standing crops in the fields, and they killed the old people and small children who were not worth capturing. In fact, some of the Pueblo Indian legends about the enemy Indians are so terrible that they are hard to believe. Probably the Indian towns were strengthened, and the walls built thicker and higher, to protect their inhabitants from the Athapascan raiders.

Apparently, the Athapascans realized the value of the Anasazi craftsmen. They married the women and made them make baskets and pottery and grind corn as well as they could in such a roving life. The Anasazi men taught the Athapascan women how to make cloth. Probably that was one way of showing the Anasazi men that they had been poor fighters and had lost. They were considered to be disgraced by doing what the Athapascans thought of as women's work.

About the year A.D. 1250, the Athapascans came sweeping down out of Montana and Idaho and Oregon and Washington to attack the cities of the Four Corners. In 1276, the Anasazi began to move south, along the Rio Grande, to the country where they now live. It is pretty certain that one of their reasons for moving was to get away from the bandits.

Another reason may have been the Great Drought that began at about that date. This drought lasted for thirty years, and dried up many of the springs and streams in the Anasazi country. While the drought must have made life in the Four Corners pretty uncomfortable, the drought was probably not the only reason why the Anasazi moved. After all, they had gone through long dry spells before. The drought alone would not have been enough to make the Anasazi want to leave their homes, but the drought combined with enemy raids was a different thing.

There may have been another cause for the Anasazi's moving, although we are not yet sure about it. It is just possible that the Indians left their homes for religious reasons. They may have thought that bad spirits had entered their country and pushed out the good ones; or they may have believed that when a cycle of life was ended the time had come to move on. And if the end of the cycle came when the bad spirits were in power—the Athapascans were attacking, and the rivers and fields were drying up—there would have been four good reasons to go. When we remember that in the Anasazi world all magical things went by fours, we can easily understand why the Indians left their country in the mountains and once again followed the rivers southward.

So, traveling a little way at a time, stopping to rest for a night or a year and going on again, the Anasazi spread south and west, down the San Juan, Colorado, and Rio Grande to the place where it bends to flow east instead of south. They went west into the mesa country of eastern Arizona. In the years between 1276 and 1400, the Anasazi settled in many new places and began to build many new towns. Some of the late Anasazi towns are in ruins now, and others are still occupied by living Indians.

The new Anasazi country looked very much like the territory the Indians had left. It was high above sea level, and its climate was dry. The valleys were ringed by mountains on which snow gathered in the winters and from which it melted in the spring. The lowlands were fertile and well watered, although they would have to be cleared of brush before crops could be planted. There was plenty of stone and adobe for building. The wild plants were those the Indians had known in their old homes; there was clay for pottery, and the only neighbors were peaceful tribes far to the south, with whom the Anasazi had probably traded for centuries. The Athapascans made occasional raids into the southern country, but on the whole the Anasazi lived peacefully and prosperously again for 266 years.

At the same time across the Atlantic Ocean Europeans had built their great cities and developed and perfected their agriculture in the same period that the Anasazi were busy doing the same things. While the Indians wanted to live peacefully and to share their goods with one another, many of the Europeans seem to have enjoyed fighting, and each of them wanted to get as much as he could for himself.

In 1492, a European named Christopher Columbus sailed from Cadiz, the most western port of Spain, the most western country of Europe, looking for gold and pearls and spices and slaves and other wealth on the mainland of Asia. Spain had fought many wars, had spent a great deal of money, and had lost many men in the two and a half centuries since the Anasazi left the Four Corners. Manpower and goods were badly needed to make Spain a self-sufficient and important country.

Columbus landed on one of the large islands east of the American mainland. He found a little gold and a few pearls and some spices the Europeans had never tasted before. Also, Columbus found Indians who were peaceful and friendly. He took them as slaves and carried them back to Spain in his ships. The old records say that "the sight of the strangers occasioned much wonder at the court."

If Columbus could do it, so could other adventurers. They sailed westward from Spain, and twenty-eight years later, in 1520, Hernando Cortés conquered the great Indian empire: Mexico to the south of the Anasazi country.

Probably the Anasazi had traded with the Mexican Indians long before they left the Four Corners country. Perhaps the ideas of agriculture and pottery and cotton cloth had come to the Anasazi from Mexico in the first place. Possibly the northern Indians got some of their religious ideas from the people to the south of them. They surely must have visited back and forth and have known something about each other for many centuries.

In Mexico the Spaniards found much gold and silver and many precious stones. They found cloth made of feathers and magnificent jeweled feather headdresses. They discovered the riches of the New World, but the invaders also found Indians who fought fiercely to protect their homes, their customs, and their lands. The Mexican Indians were not easy to capture and enslave. After many battles some of them were conquered.

The others hid in the mountains, where they could not be found. Some may even have escaped across the desert to the north, bringing Aztec words on their tongues to teach the Anasazi.

After the Spaniards had captured much of Mexico, they asked where the largest and richest cities of the country were located. The Mexican Indians pointed northward with their chins, and answered, in Spanish, "*Mas alla* (mahs ah-YAH)," which means, "Further on." The Spaniards hurried on the way northward then, looking for more gold and more silver, more feather cloth, more precious stones, and always for more slaves.

It all happened so long ago that probably nobody will ever know exactly why the Mexican Indians pointed the Spaniards northward. Perhaps the southern people honestly believed that those in the north were richer than themselves and were afraid not to tell the Spaniards about them. Perhaps the Indians were only guessing about it. Or perhaps someone from the Valley of Mexico had once gone north to Arizona to trade, had seen the stone and mud towns there, and knew how simply the Anasazi lived. If that Mexican Indian had made the journey, he knew about the desert country of Chihuahua (chee-WAH-wah) and Sonora (soe-NOE-rah), which the Spaniards would have to cross. The Mexican Indian probably hoped the invaders would all die of lack of water or at the hands of the Yaquis (YAH-kees).

The Spaniards might have given up when they reached the desert, if they had not encountered one of their former slaves. This man was a Negro from the north of Africa, what the Spaniards called a Moor, and his name was Esteban, or Stephen. He had been with a group of Spaniards who had landed on the west coast of Florida. The Indians there had attacked the strangers and killed everyone but Esteban and one Spaniard. The two of them traveled west and south, looking for other Spaniards, and they must have walked all the way across Louisiana and Texas, southern New Mexico, and parts of Mexico. Esteban said that he knew where there were seven great Indian cities to the north. He said they were called Cíbola (SEE-boe-lah), which is the Spanish word for buffalo, and that east of Cíbola there was another cluster of towns, the group being named Quivira (kee-VEE-rah).

So Esteban guided the Spaniards northward across the desert, almost to Zuni Pueblo. There he was killed. The Indians may have recognized him and hoped that they could drive all the Spaniards away—back to Mexico, back to the Caribbean Islands, back across the sea to Spain.

By that time it was too late. There were more Indians than there were Spaniards, but the Spaniards had better weapons than the Indians. Instead of stone knives and darts with stone points, the Spanish soldiers were armed with steel swords and bayonets and daggers. Instead of plain bows and arrows, the Spaniards carried crossbows, which are even more powerful than sinew-backed bows. And, most important of all, the Spaniards had horses.

The first time the Indians saw a horse equipped with a heavy military saddle and plate armor, with a man on its back also in armor, they thought they were seeing a strange and wonderful animal. When they saw the animal stop and the man get off and walk about on his own two feet, the Indians thought the magic animal had split itself in two. They ran into their houses and barred the doors, for they were terrified of such a spirit-being. It was a long time before the Spaniards let the Indians know that a horse was just another animal, and that it, and the person who rode it, could be killed.

With their horses and armor, the Spaniards conquered the Indians with very little real fighting. The strangers brought in their own government officials and their own priests, and took control of the country. The Spaniards said that the Indians were to be their slaves and work for the conquerors; and they beat and whipped and sometimes killed them if they did not obey. They also insisted that the Indians give up their own religion and be baptized Christians.

Beginning with the time of the Spanish conquest, the Indians kept secrets from the outsiders. If the Spaniards had come to the Southwest as visitors and had been polite and friendly, the Indians would probably have treated them as well as they did well-behaved strangers from other tribes. They would have fed the newcomers and given them houses to live in and clothes to wear. They would probably have given the Spaniards all the gold and silver, and most of the turquoise, they had, for the Indians thought these things were beautiful but not as valuable as fine baskets and blankets and pottery and corn. And probably the Indians would have asked the Spaniards to worship with them and would have welcomed them into the kivas.

None of these things happened. The Spaniards attacked and mistreated the Indians. The Indians in the towns along the Rio Grande stood it as long as they could. Then they organized the First American Revolution.

At night, messengers went along the river trails and across the mesas from one town to the next. Men slipped through the rows of cornstalks in their fields, hid in the high brush along the streams, crawled up mountains and along high ridges, and got away in broad daylight. One at a time, and then a few at a time, the Anasazi rebels went from town to town and made their secret plans. The leader of the rebellion was Popé (poe-PAY), a man from Taos, which is the most northern and eastern and the fiercest of the pueblos. Popé directed the messengers to carry knotted strings to the *caciques* of all the Rio Grande towns. Some of the Athapascan chiefs were told what was afoot, and they agreed to join the Anasazi against the Spaniards. Every day each *cacique* and each chief was to untie one knot in his string. On the day when the strings hung loose and straight, it was the time to attack the Spaniards.

The secret was kept. Weapons were gathered and preparations made until the day before the last string was to be untied. Then a man from San Juan Pueblo turned traitor and confessed the whole plan to a Spanish priest. The Spaniards attacked the Indians again, but this time the Indians were ready for them. They drove the Spaniards south and out into the desert, where many of them died. The Indians hung the men they captured, or burned them at the stake, or strangled them. They took their own country back and governed it in their own way for twelve years.

Enough Spaniards had escaped and made their way to Mexico City to tell the military government there what had happened. In 1692, an expedition was sent out to recapture New Mexico and Arizona. The expedition was large and well armed, and eventually it was successful. The Spaniards overcame the Indians again, and this time they conquered and controlled the whole Southwest.

The names of the Indian towns were changed. Waters Meeting Place became San Ildefonso. Town on the Bluff was called San Juan of the Cavaliers. Roses Growing Near the Water was renamed Santa Clara. Only a few of the towns— Round Valley, and Cottonwoods Grow Tall, and Rainbow House People Town—kept their Indian names: Nambé, Tesuque, Taos.

The Indian people were renamed, too, and were ordered to use only their Spanish names under penalty of death. So Long Cloud over the Mesa took the name of Júlian Martinez, and his wife, Yellow Pond Lily Blooming, became María Antonia Martinez. But still, even though they called each other Júlian and María, each had an Indian name which was often used.

The Spaniards insisted that all Indian babies should be baptized. They required all adults to get permission from the military or civil authorities before they married, and to be married in the church. For a while the Indians had to hold their own marriage ceremonies in secret; later, they worked out a way of combining the church and Indian wedding ceremonies. The Spaniards also ordered the Indians to bury their dead in the churchyards, as Europeans of that day were buried. A few Indians obeyed, but many more hid the bodies of their dead, and laid them secretly on the mountaintops, as they were accustomed to doing.

The Spaniards did not destroy the kivas, but they did force

the Indians to build great mission churches. On Acoma Mesa,
three hundred feet above the valley where the Indians of
Acoma Pueblo have their farms, such a church was built.
Before it could be constructed, earth and sand to make adobe
bricks and mortar, and stones to reinforce the walls, had to
be carried a basketful at a time from the river bottoms, for
the top of the mesa is a solid sheet of rock. The people
carried the materials and the water to mix with them on their
heads. They built not only a church but a churchyard a block
square and eight feet deep, with a four-foot-high adobe wall
around it, in front of the church.

In Chimayó Valley, east of the Rio Grande, there was a tiny
pueblo. Nearby there was a spring, and the Indians believed
that the spring and the earth from which it flowed were sacred
and magical and could heal sickness. The Spaniards built a
shrine above the spring and told the Indians they could still
worship there if they wanted to, but they must worship the
Christian God instead of the nature spirits. The Indians still
go to the shrine of Chimayó to pray.

A few of the Indians learned to read and write after the
Spaniards came. More learned to use metal hoes and spades

and axes, to break their fields with plows, and to care for horses, cattle, sheep, goats, pigs, chickens, ducks, and geese. They learned what money was, and that if they worked hard for their masters they might be given a little of it, to trade at the master's store for tools and cloth.

The Indians learned to plant wheat, rye, barley, cabbage, onions, garlic, lettuce, radishes, and peas in their gardens. The Spaniards also brought them plants from other parts of the New World, like chile peppers and tomatoes and potatoes, and taught them how to raise those. There were orchards of peaches, pears, apples, apricots, and European plums. Many new foods were planted, but the Indians still raised corn and beans and squashes. After a while, the Spaniards learned to use the native vegetables as the Indians did.

The Indian women changed their ways less than the men did, at first. They liked their corn ground on metates, and even when the Spaniards built water mills to grind the grain, the women continued to make most of their cornmeal at home. If they wanted wheat flour, the women sometimes had it ground on the new-fangled machines, but just as often they made it themselves on the grinding stones in their own kitchens. Indian pottery was easier to get and as satisfactory to use as European dishes and metal cooking pots, so for a long time the kitchens were almost unchanged. The one Spanish introduction the women were delighted with, and began to use almost immediately, was the chimney. As soon as they learned how to build tubes to carry the smoke out of the houses, the women began constructing them.

The Indian women also liked woolen cloth, and soon woolen dresses and blankets replaced cotton ones on the Anasazi looms. Wool is easier to spin and faster to weave than cotton, and the men enjoyed working with it. They liked the Spanish indigo blue and brazilwood brown dyes, and they especially liked the cochineal red dye they made from raveled Spanish cloth. The Indians had more colorful clothing after the Spanish conquest than they had ever seen before.

After a time, things more or less settled down in the

Southwest. The Spaniards fought with the Athapascans, for they wanted to protect the fields they had captured and the Indians who worked in the fields for them. The Indians observed the new religion on Sundays and feast days, and their own the rest of the time. Some of the Spanish soldiers started farming, and more farmers moved in from Spain and from the other Spanish colonies. Some of the Spaniards married Indian women. Others brought their wives from Mexico or Spain, and decided to live peaceably with their families. The Indians learned Spanish, although they continued to use their own languages at home among themselves. The two peoples managed to live peacefully side by side.

Then Spain grew weaker and lost her power in Europe and in the New World. In the early 1800s, the people of Mexico rebelled against the Spaniards and established their own independent government. They followed the example of the English colonies along the Atlantic Coast—the same ones that became the first United States of America. The Mexican government proclaimed that its territory included what is now Texas, New Mexico, Arizona, California, Utah, Colorado, Nevada, and part of Oklahoma, but it could send only a few officials and soldiers to administer that part of the country and fight off the Athapascans. The lives of the Pueblo Indians changed very little when Mexico became an independent nation.

In 1846, a war was fought between the United States and Mexico. When a peace agreement was signed, the United States claimed all the territory north of the Rio Grande, and it took over the Four Corners country and the villages along the Rio Grande. American soldiers and governors were sent into the Southwest. This time they brought cheap cotton trade cloth, and more knives and axes, and brass buckets, and glass beads to trade to the Indians for corn and beans and squash seeds and dried meat and fruit.

Still the lives of the Indians remained about the same. President Lincoln recognized the right of each village to own and use the land it occupied, and he sent a gold-headed cane to each Indian governor to seal the agreement. The Indians promised to stay at home and mind their own business, as they had always done, and the American officials promised that in exchange for a large share of the Indian land they would build schools and hospitals and would see that the Indians received justice in the courts.

One other great change took place in the Anasazi country in the late 1800s and early 1900s. Lumber companies came into the Southwest and began to cut the timber on the high mountains. The great trees whose roots had held the soil together and had helped retain moisture in the soil were cut down. Now when the summer rains came, or the snows melted in the spring, the water poured off the mountains, carrying the earth with it. The Indian towns were flooded when the rivers rose in the rains or thaws, and the cornfields and bean gardens were destroyed. The Indians suffered greatly because they lacked food.

New diseases came into the Indian country with the newcomers. Measles and whooping cough and tuberculosis and smallpox and other diseases had been unknown until Europeans brought them. Not even the newcomers, who had known about these sicknesses for so many centuries that they were no longer much affected by them, knew how to treat them medically. The Indians, who had never known such epidemics, were helpless. Thousands of them died from chicken pox and mumps and pneumonia which their priests did not know how to cure.

The time came when there were only a very few poor Indians left in the villages along the Rio Grande. Then some of the Americans saw what was happening and began working to change conditions. About 1920 more hospitals were built and more doctors were sent to the pueblos, to keep the promise President Lincoln had made to the Indian governors. New schools were built, and more children had a chance to go to them and to learn to read and write. Most important of all, much of the timberland was declared to be part of the public domain, which means the land belongs to all the

Indian Designs	European Designs	Time
		A.D. 11 to A.D. 300
		A.D. 300 to A.D. 500
		A.D. 500 to A.D. 700
		A.D. 700 to A.D. 1050
		A.D. 1050 to A.D. 1300
		A.D. 1300 to A.D. 1539
		A.D. 1540 A.D. 1680 A.D. 1692 A.D. 1804 A.D. 1812 A.D. 1846

and European History

What Happened in the Southwest	What Happened in the Old World
Wandering seed gatherers and hunters reached the Four Corners. They lived in brush shelters, stored their food in pits, and cooked in baskets. They hunted with atlatls and nets.	Christianity developed and spread in the Mediterranean world. The Romans conquered and occupied the British Isles.
Hunting and gathering continued, and the people also learned to grow corn and beans. They lived in pit houses, with built-in metates and storage pits. They made fine blankets, sandals, and fur cloth.	The Roman Empire fell, and the Dark Ages began. Parts of great churches, like St. Peter's at Rome, were built. The crossbow was introduced from the Orient. Legends of King Arthur were told for the first time.
Pit house towns were built in caves. Beans were planted. Bows and arrows were introduced. The first true pottery was made.	The Saxons built stone towns in England. Learning centered in the churches and convents, while the kings fought each other.
Houses were built above ground and in the open. Storehouses and dwellings were separate. Walled towns developed. Kivas were built. Cotton was introduced. Turkeys were domesticated.	The Middle Ages began with the reign of Charlemagne. Trade goods were organized by the business people. Leif Eriksson landed on the East Coast of America.
Great terraced cities were built in caves or on mesas. Weaving and pottery reached their highest development. The Great Drought began in 1276, and people began to move south, out of the Four Corners.	The Middle Ages were the time of the Crusades. William of Normandy conquered England in 1066. Marco Polo visited China and brought back the ship's compass. Modern science began.
Towns, some of them still occupied, were built in the Rio Grande and in Arizona. Glaze-point decoration was applied to pottery. News of the Spanish conquest of Mexico spread northward.	The Renaissance began. Chimneys and glass windows were invented, as were portable guns. The first book, the Gutenberg Bible, was printed in 1453. Columbus arrived in the New World.

Coronado invaded and conquered the Southwest.
The Pueblo Indians rebelled against the Spaniards.
The Spaniards reconquered the Southwest.
The Lewis and Clark Expedition occurred.
Mexico gained its independence from Spain.
The United States defeated Mexico and gained control of the Southwest.

people of the United States, both Indians and non-Indians. No man, or company of men, could cut any more timber without an official government permit, and without planting new trees to replace those they chopped down. Diversion dams and baffles were built to protect the Indians' fields. This time there was a change for the better.

As it had in the old times, when corn was introduced the Indian population began to increase. More babies were born and survived, and the old people lived longer. Health improved, and the walls of the houses were repaired. The people had better shelter. Life was now better, after all the centuries of oppression and sorrow.

MODERN TIMES

THE INDIAN pueblos of today stretch along the Rio Grande and across the Arizona mesas like shell beads on a sinew cord. From Taos and Picuris in the north, through Isleta south of Albuquerque, on westward from Laguna to the farthest Hopi town, they stand strong and solid; earth colored; surrounded by green fields and gardens.

If you visit one of these Indian towns, you will notice three things right away. The town is always clean; the plaza is swept; and the adobe plaster on the house walls is smooth. You feel that this spotless town is very quiet, and that no one who lives there hurries or speaks sharply. And when a person comes from one of the houses to meet you, and to tell you where to park and what houses you may enter, he is always polite because you are a stranger in his town. He is probably the governor or one of his assistants.

If you are invited into an Indian house, you enter a room that is as clean as the plaza outside. The woman who opens the door at your knock smiles at you and asks you to come in and sit down. She will show you her pottery, if you ask to see it, and she will sell you a piece if she has any to spare. You sit on a chair, and perhaps through the open door you can see a kitchen with a coal or bottled-gas cooking stove and the metates that are set into the floor between the stove and a mouse-proof steel cupboard. The rafters of the living room are so old that the marks of the ax that stripped off the bark ripple the surface of the wood, but from the herringbone ceiling of aspen or cedar poles there hangs an electric lightbulb. The Indians are proud of their homes, and do all they can to make their houses comfortable.

If you are visiting the pueblo on a feast day, you may be asked to have dinner with an Indian family. The women have spent at least four days preparing for the meal, and everything is ready to entertain their visitors. Long board tables are set in the living room, and have been covered with bright new oilcloth. China dishes, and metal knives, forks, and spoons are set at each place.

The dinner that is served includes both old and new foods. There is sure to be dried meat cooked with hominy and seasoned with chile. There will be dried fruit stewed soft and sweetened with honey. There will be tamales, and bowls of *atole*, and trays of *piki* bread. There are sure to be beans and squash and corn on the cob, or stewed dried corn. There will also be pitchers of milk, and pots of coffee for the grown-ups, and pie and cake. Often there are big bowls of potato salad and coleslaw and canned fruit salad. And there are bowls of popcorn and piles of cookies and candies and apples and oranges, from the store, to be given to the children.

When you go to the plaza, after dinner, you will see one of the old, old Indian dances, and will listen to the old, old songs. The drummer may beat time on a drum that has been kept in the kiva for hundreds of years. The clothes the dancers wear have been handed down from one generation to another ever since the Indians began to spin and weave with wool.

Many of the Indians who watch the dancing sit on the bumpers or running boards of their pickup trucks or station wagons. An old lady may cross the plaza, carrying *piki* bread in an enamel dishpan, on her way to the kiva with food for the dancers. The young people who help her with her load have been away to school in the government boarding schools, and some of them may even be college graduates who work in the non-Indian towns near the pueblo.

Perhaps some of the men are war veterans, for Indians will still fight if their country is attacked. Perhaps the dance itself is given in honor of a young man who has returned safely from war.

If you have brought your camera and want to take pictures, you ask permission from one of the Indian policemen who stand, wrapped in beautiful, striped, soft woolen blankets on the sides of the plaza, and keep visitors from getting too near the dancers. Perhaps the guard tells you that this is not a sacred dance and that you may photograph it if you pay a fee.

Outside the plaza is the church, and you may go to see it. Inside, the church is very plain. The floor is made of boards, and there are a few narrow plank benches. The walls are whitewashed above and painted with colored-earth bands below. In some Indian churches pictures copied from those in the kivas have been painted on the walls. The figures of saints that stand on the church altar are often very old. They were carved from cottonwood limbs a hundred years ago, and their faces and clothing are painted on with earth colors. Perhaps some women, with shawls drawn over their heads, kneel on the floor before the altar. You tiptoe out, so as not to disturb their prayers.

On feast days the Indians dance and sing and eat and enjoy themselves. They are happy, and they want their visitors to share their happiness and the blessing of the dance.

On other days the Indians work hard. Some of the men are farmers, who must go into their fields at sunrise and work till dark during the growing season. Others have jobs in the non-Indian towns. Perhaps they get up early and drive to work in the family car, or perhaps they stay in town all week and come home to visit their families on weekends. A few of the oldest men have no regular jobs. Their time for hard work is over. They sit in the sun on bright days, talking, telling the old stories and singing the old songs, repeating their customs to each other and to the little boys. Some days the

The Old and the New at Taos Pueblo

old men take the boys into the kiva and give them lessons in the ways and the history of their people there, as Indian grandfathers have always done.

The women care for their houses and families. They cook and sew, and wash clothes with yucca suds or with soap from the store. They teach their daughters to grind cornmeal on the metates and to use a sink to wash the dishes. They sing the housekeeping songs and tell the history stories while they work, and the girls listen and learn from their mothers the things that Indian women need to know today.

Whatever tasks occupy them, the Indians sing. There are still songs to go with every chore. In the evenings, when the day's work is finished and the family sits down by the fire in the living room to rest a little before bedtime, someone is almost sure to bring out a hand drum and tap in time to a little song.

HOME SONG

My mother's house
My father's fields
Are all around me.
The ways of my people
From the oldest times
They are around me, too.
The sun is over us.
The moon is over us.
The stars shine on us.
The earth is beneath us.
They bless us all.
Corn grows in our fields,
Deer run on the mountains,
The snow melts into the rivers,

And the clouds gather to bring us rain.
All these things bless us.
We are rich in blessings.
We hold our blessings close
And open our arms
To share our blessings with all people.

BIBLIOGRAPHY

Adair, John. *The Navajo and Pueblo Silversmiths.* Norman: University of Oklahoma Press, 1944.

Amsden, Charles Avery. *Prehistoric Southwesterners from Basketmaker to Pueblo.* Los Angeles: Southwest Museum, 1949.

Arizona (State) Highway Department. *Arizona Highways Magazine.* Prescott, Ariz.: The Department.

Astrov, Margot. *The Winged Serpent.* New York: John Day Company, 1946.

Bancroft, Henry Howe. *History of Arizona and New Mexico.* San Francisco: Golden West Publishing Company, 1889.

Bandelier, Adolf F. *The Delight Makers.* New York: Dodd, Mead, and Company, 1926.

Bolton, Herbert Eugene, ed. *Spanish Exploration of the Southwest, 1542–1706.* New York: Charles Scribner's Sons, 1916.

Bunzel, Ruth L. *Zuni Ritual Poetry.* Bureau of American Ethnology 47th Annual Report. Washington, D.C.: Government Printing Office, 1932.

Chapman, Kenneth M. *Pueblo Indian Pottery of the Post-Spanish Period.* 2d ed.　　Santa Fe, N.M.: Laboratory of Anthropology, 1945.

Colton, Harold S. "The Patayan Problem in the Colorado River Valley." *Southwest Journal of Anthropology* 1, no. 1 (1945).

Curtis, Natalie. *The Indians' Book.* New York: Harper and Brothers, 1935.

Cushing, Frank Hamilton. *My Adventures in Zuni.* Santa Fe, N.M.: Peripatetic Press, 1941.

————. *Outlines of Zuni Creation Myths.* Bureau of American Ethnology 13th Annual Report, 1891–1892. Washington, D.C.: Government Printing Office, 1896.

Douglas, Frederic H. *Pottery of the Southwestern Tribes.* "Indian Leaflets Series," nos. 69, 70. Denver, Colo.: Denver Art Museum, 1935.

————. *Modern Pueblo Pottery Types.* "Indian Leaflets Series," nos. 53, 54. Denver, Colo.: Denver Art Museum, 1933.

————. *Santa Clara and San Juan Pottery.* "Indian Leaflets Series," no. 35. Denver, Colo.: Denver Art Museum, 1931.

_____ . *Periods of Pueblo Culture and History.* "Indian Leaflets Series," no. 17. Denver, Colo.: Denver Art Museum, 1930.

_____ . *Pueblo Indian Pottery Making.* "Indian Leaflets Series," no. 6. Denver, Colo.: Denver Art Museum, 1930.

_____ . *Southwestern Indian Dwellings.* "Indian Leaflets Series," no. 9. Denver, Colo.: Denver Art Museum, 1930.

Douglas, Frederic H., and Rene d'Harnoncourt. *Indian Art of the United States.* New York: Museum of Modern Art, 1941.

Eickmeyer, Carl, and Lillian L. Eickmeyer. *Among the Pueblo Indians.* New York: Merriam and Company, 1895.

Exposition of Indian Tribal Arts. *Introduction to American Indian Art,* parts 1 and 2. New York: The Exposition, 1931.

Fewkes, Jesse Walter. *Designs on Prehistoric Hopi Pottery.* Bureau of American Ethnology 33rd Annual Report, 1911–1912. Washington, D.C.: Government Printing Office, 1919.

_____ . *Prehistoric Villages, Castles, and Towers of Southwestern Colorado.* Bureau of American Ethnology Bulletin 70. Washington, D.C.: Government Printing Office, 1919.

_____ . *Antiquities of the Mesa Verde National Park: Cliff Palace.* Bureau of American Ethnology Bulletin 51. Washington, D.C.: Government Printing Office, 1911.

_____ . *Antiquities of the Mesa Verde National Park: Spruce Tree House.* Bureau of American Ethnology Bulletin 41. Washington, D.C.: Government Printing Office, 1909.

Field, Dorothy. "Notes on Jemez Pueblo." Manuscript.

"Fine Exhibit of Pottery." *El Palacio,* 8, nos. 7, 8 (July 1920).

Garrard, Lewis H. *Wah-To-Yah and the Taos Trail.* Edited by Stanley Vestal. Oklahoma City, Okla.: Harlow Publishing Company, 1927.

Gilpin, Laura. *The Pueblos.* New York: Hastings House, 1940.

Goddard, Pliny Earle. *Indians of the Southwest.* 4th ed. New York: American Museum of Natural History, 1931.

Guthe, Carl E. *Pueblo Pottery Making.* Papers, Phillips Academy Southwestern Expedition, no. 2. New Haven, Conn.: Yale University Press, 1925.

Hall, Ansel F. *Mesa Verde.* Mancos, Colo.: Ansel F. Hall, 1951.

Halseth, Odd S. "Revival of Pueblo Pottery-Making." *El Palacio,* 21, no. 6 (September 15, 1926).

Harding, Anne, and Patricia Bolling. *Bibliography of Articles and Papers on North American Indian Art.* Washington, D.C.: United States Department of the Interior, 1938.

Harrington, John P. *Ethnogeography of the Tewa Indians.* Bureau of American Ethnology 29th Annual Report, 1907–1908. Washington, D.C.: Government Printing Office, 1916.

Haury, Emil W. *Painted Cave, Northeastern Arizona.* Dragoon, Ariz.: Amerindian Foundation, 1945.

Hawley, Florence M. "The Role of Pueblo Social Organization in the Dissemination of Catholicism." *American Anthropologist* 48, no. 3 (1946).

————. "Pueblo Social Organization as a Lead to Pueblo History." *American Anthropologist* 39, no. 3, (1937).

Hendron, J. W. *Prehistory of El Rito de los Frijoles, Bandelier National Monument.* Coolidge, Ariz.: National Monuments Association, 1940.

Hewett, Edgar L. *Ancient Life in the American Southwest.* New York: Tudor Publishing Company, 1943.

————. *Pajarito Plateau and Its Ancient People.* Albuquerque: University of New Mexico Press, 1938.

————. *Excavations at El Rito de los Frijoles in 1909.* Papers of the School of American Archaeology, no. 10. Reprinted from *American Anthropologist* 11, no. 4 (October–December 1909).

————. *Excavations at Tuyonyi, New Mexico, in 1908.* Papers of the School of American Archaeology, no. 5. Reprinted from *American Anthropologist* 11, no. 3 (July–September 1909).

————. *The Puye.* Papers of the School of American Research, no. 4. Santa Fe, N.M.: Museum of New Mexico, n.d.

Hodge, Frederick W., ed. *Handbook of American Indians North of Mexico.* Bureau of American Ethnology Bulletin 30. Washington, D.C.: Government Printing Office, 1910.

Jackson, John B. "Human Geography of the Southwest." Manuscript.

Jackson, John B., ed. *Landscape: Human Geography of the Southwest.* Santa Fe, N.M.: n.p., 1951.

Kelemen, Pal. *Medieval American Art.* New York: Macmillan Company, 1943.

Kidder, Alfred V. *Pottery of Pecos.* Andover, N.H.: Phillips Academy, 1931.

————. *Southwestern Archaeology.* New Haven, Conn.: Yale University Press, 1924.

Kubler, George. *The Religious Architecture of New Mexico.* Colorado Springs, Colo.: Taylor Museum, 1940.

Lockett, H. C., and Milton Snow. *Along the Beale Trail.* 2d. ed. Lawrence, Kan.: Haskell Institute Press, 1940.

McGregor, John C. *Southwestern Archaeology.* New York: John Wiley and Sons Company, 1941.

Marriott, Alice. *These Are the People.* Santa Fe, N.M.: Museum of New Mexico Press, 1951.

————. *The Valley Below.* Norman: University of Oklahoma Press, 1949.

————. *Maria: The Potter of San Ildefonso.* Norman: University of Oklahoma Press, 1948.

————. *Indians on Horseback.* New York: Thomas Y. Crowell Company, 1948.

Mera, Harry P. "Negative Painting on Southwestern Pottery." *Southwest Journal of Anthropology* 1, no. 1 (1945).

————. *Style Trends in Pueblo Pottery.* Santa Fe, N.M.: Laboratory of Anthropology, 1939.

_____. *Reconnaissance and Excavation in Southwestern New Mexico.* American Anthropological Association Memoirs, no. 51. Menasha, Wis.: American Anthropological Association, 1939.

_____. *The "Rain Bird": A Study in Pueblo Design.* Santa Fe, N.M.: Laboratory of Anthropology, 1937.

Meriam, Lewis, et al. *The Problem of Indian Administration.* Report of a Survey Made at the Request of the Secretary of the Interior. (Institute for Government Research, Studies in Administration.) Baltimore, Md.: Johns Hopkins University Press, 1928.

Mindeleff, Cosmos. *Aboriginal Remains in Verde Valley, Arizona.* Bureau of American Ethnology 13th Annual Report, 1891–1892. Washington, D.C.: Government Printing Office, 1896.

_____. *Casa Grande Ruin.* Bureau of American Ethnology 13th Annual Report, 1891–1892. Washington, D.C.: Government Printing Office, 1896.

Mindeleff, Victor. *Study of Pueblo Architecture.* Bureau of American Ethnology 8th Annual Report, 1886–1887. Washington, D.C.: Government Printing Office, 1891.

Morley, Sylvanus Griswold. *The South House, Puye.* Papers of the School of American Archaeology, no. 7. Santa Fe, N.M.: Museum of New Mexico Press, 1909(?).

Morris, Ann Axtell. *Digging in the Southwest.* New York: Doubleday, 1933.

Morris, Earl H. *Preliminary Report of the Antiquities of the Region between the Mancos and La Plata Rivers in Southwestern Colorado.* Bureau of American Ethnology 33rd Annual Report, 1911–1912. Washington, D.C.: Government Printing Office, 1919.

O'Kane, Walter Collins. *Sun in the Sky: The Hopi Indians of the Arizona Mesa Lands.* Norman: University of Oklahoma Press, 1950.

Prince, L. Bradford. *A Concise History of New Mexico.* 2d. ed. Cedar Rapids, Ia.: Torch Press, 1914.

Reed, Erik K. "Aspects of Acculturation in the Southwest." *Acta American,* 2, nos. 1, 2 (1944).

Roberts, Frank H. H., Jr. "Survey of Southwestern Archaeology." *American Anthropologist* 37, no. 1 (1935).

_____. *Shabik'eshchee Village.* Bureau of American Ethnology Bulletin 92. Washington, D.C.: Government Printing Office, 1929.

Sims, Agnes C. *San Cristobal Petroglyphs.* Santa Fe, N.M.: Pictograph Press, 1949.

Smithsonian Institution. *Explorations and Field Work in 1912, 1913, 1914.* Washington, D.C.: Government Printing Office, 1914.

Spinden, Herbert Joseph. *Songs of the Tewa.* New York: Exposition of Indian Tribal Arts, 1933.

_____. "The Making of Pottery at San Ildefonso." *American Museum Journal* 11, no. 6 (October 1911).

Stevenson, James. *Illustrated Catalog of Specimens Obtained from the Indians of New Mexico and Arizona in 1879.* Bureau of American Ethnology 2nd Annual Report, 1880–1881. Washington, D.C.: Government Printing Office, 1882.

Stevenson, Matilda C. "Pueblo Clothing." Manuscript now at Bureau of American Ethnology.

Stubbs, Stanley A. *Bird's-Eye View of the Pueblos.* Norman: University of Oklahoma Press, 1950.

Underhill, Ruth Murray. *Pueblo Crafts.* Phoenix, Ariz.: Phoenix Indian School, 1946.

United States, Department of Interior, National Park Service. *Mesa Verde National Park, Colorado.* Washington, D.C.: Government Printing Office, 1948.

United States, Office of Indian Affairs. *Indians at Work.* Washington, D.C.: United States Indian Service, 1934–1943.

Vaillant, George C. *Indian Arts in North America.* New York: Harper and Brothers, 1939.

Whitman, William. *The Pueblo Indians of San Ildefonso.* New York: Columbia University Press, 1946.

Wissler, Clark. *The American Indian.* 3d. ed. New York: Oxford University Press, 1938.

Wormington, H. Marie. *Prehistoric Indians of the Southwest.* Denver, Colo.: Denver Museum of Natural History, 1947.

Wormington, H. Marie, and Arminta Neal. *Story of Pueblo Pottery.* Denver, Colo.: Denver Museum of Natural History, 1951.

INDEX

Other Titles in this Series

Ancient City Press
P.O. Box 5401
Santa Fe, New Mexico 87502
(505) 982-8195